THE GREAT BIG BOOK OF GAMES AND PUZZLES

THE GREAT BIG BOOK OF GAMES AND PUZZLES

ARCTURUS

ARCTURUS

This edition published in 2009 by Arcturus Publishing Limited
26/27 Bickels Yard, 151–153 Bermondsey Street,
London SE1 3HA

ISBN: 978-1-84837-357-0
CH000631US

Printed in Singapore

Design and Illustration by CREATIVE QUOTIENT

Compiler: Anna Amari-Parker
Editor: Rebecca Gerlings

Contents

Inside Games 9-20

Chain Reaction - 10
Bowling with Marbles - - - - - - - - - - - - - - - - - 11
Hot Hands - 12
Musical Chairs - 13
Banana, Knife, and Fork - - - - - - - - - - - - - - 14
The Waiter - 16
Human Chairs - 17
Tchuka Ruma - 18
The Ice-Skating Rink - - - - - - - - - - - - - - - - 20

Outside Games 21-32

King (or Queen!) of the Hill - - - - - - - - - - - - 22
Red Light, Green Light - - - - - - - - - - - - - - - 23
Hunter and Watchman - - - - - - - - - - - - - - - 24
Capture the Flag - - - - - - - - - - - - - - - - - - - 26
Hole in One - 28
Beanbag Toss - 29
Dodge Ball - 30
Tug of War - 31
Triangular Tug of War - - - - - - - - - - - - - - - 32

Races and Relays 33-42

Racing Bunnies - 34
Three-Legged Race - - - - - - - - - - - - - - - - - 35
Twisted Arms Race - - - - - - - - - - - - - - - - - 36
Egg and Spoon Race - - - - - - - - - - - - - - - - 38
Wheelbarrow Race - - - - - - - - - - - - - - - - - 39
Piggyback Race - 40
Crab Relay - 41
Pass the Orange Race - - - - - - - - - - - - - - - 42

Hunts and Hide-and-Seeks

43-54

Ghost in the Graveyard - - - - - - - - - - - - - - - - 44
Classic Hide-and-Seek - - - - - - - - - - - - - - - - 46
Sardines - 47
Cops and Robbers - - - - - - - - - - - - - - - - - 48
Mice and Wolves - - - - - - - - - - - - - - - - - - 50
The Great Duel - - - - - - - - - - - - - - - - - - - 52
Scavenger Hunt - - - - - - - - - - - - - - - - - - 54

Party Games

55-66

Statues - 56
The Gods - 58
Pass the Parcel - - - - - - - - - - - - - - - - - - - 59
Blowing Bubbles - - - - - - - - - - - - - - - - - - 60
Pin the Tail on the Donkey - - - - - - - - - - - - 62
Simon Says - 64
Limbo Dancing - - - - - - - - - - - - - - - - - - - 66

Guessing Games

67-76

I Spy - 68
What Am I Touching? - - - - - - - - - - - - - - - 69
Pictionary - 70
Rhyming Charades - - - - - - - - - - - - - - - - 72
Who Am I? - 74
What's that Tune? - - - - - - - - - - - - - - - - - 75
Murder in the Dark - - - - - - - - - - - - - - - 76

Hand Games

77-88

Origami Challenge - - - - - - - - - - - - - - - - - 78
Paper, Scissors, Stone - - - - - - - - - - - - - - - 80
The Well - 81
String Challenge 1: The Bowl on a Plate - - - - - 82
String Challenge 2: The Eiffel Tower - - - - - - - 83
String Challenge 3: Dreamcatcher - - - - - - - - 84
String Challenge 4: The Parachute, Dad's
    Pants, Mom's Apron, Grandma's Shoes - - - - - - 86

Paper and Pencil Games

89-96

Little Monster - - - - - - - - - - - - - - - - - - - 90
Follow that Line! - - - - - - - - - - - - - - - - - - 92
Tick-Tack-Toe with Numbers - - - - - - - - - - - 94
Growing Crystals - - - - - - - - - - - - - - - - - - 96

Word Games

97–108

Antonyms - 98
Questions and Answers - - - - - - - - - - - - - - 99
Picture-Word Associations - - - - - - - - - - - 100
Spelling Bee - 102
Earth, Wind, Air, and Fire - - - - - - - - - - - 103
Word Factory - 104
Hangman - 106
Hidden Words - 108

Strategy Games

109–120

Giant Slaying - 110
The Star - 111
Fox and Geese - 112
Two-Color Snakes - - - - - - - - - - - - - - - - - - 113
Connect the Dots - - - - - - - - - - - - - - - - - - 114
Battleships - 116
Checkers - 118
3-D Noughts and Crosses - - - - - - - - - - - - 119
Halma - 120

Tabletop Games

121–126

Dominoes - 122
Pick-Up Sticks - 125
Pick-Up Toothpicks - - - - - - - - - - - - - - - - 126

Card Games

127–138

Old Maid - 128
Slapjack - 130
Fifteen - 131
War - 132
Chase the Ace - 134
Rummy - 136

Dice Games

139–144

Little Pig - 140
Nifty Fifty - 141
The Racing Clock - - - - - - - - - - - - - - - - - - 142
Multiplication Dice - - - - - - - - - - - - - - - - 143
Unlucky Dice - 144

THE GREAT BIG BOOK OF GAMES AND PUZZLES

Whether you're looking for party games, rainy day activities, or brainteasers, you're sure to find what you're after in **The Great Big Book of Games and Puzzles**.

All entries begin with a breakdown of the numbers of players and equipment required, and are arranged within each section according to their level of difficulty, so you can start the fun without delay!

KEY:

 = number of players

 = simple

 = tricky

 = challenging

 = equipment needed

 = aim of the game

Inside Games

Chain Reaction

 5 or more   1   None

 To figure out what the first player was thinking of.

1 All players stand in line looking the same way.

2 If you are first in line, at the signal to start, turn round and begin to mime the movements of an animal or an occupation as the second player looks on.

3 At the end of your turn, your neighbor will repeat your mime, facial expressions, and gestures to the third player in line and so on. This process of imitation is repeated until it is the turn of the last player in the line.

4 This player has to guess what the first player was trying to communicate from watching the performance of the player next to him or her. This game is guaranteed to be very funny because answers tend to be as far off the mark as they are off the wall!

Bowling with Marbles

 2 or more 1 6 marbles of the same color (for each player), 1 larger marble as the target, a stick of chalk for marking out the playing field

 To flick your marbles as close as possible to the target.

1 Draw a shooting line with the chalk and decide where to place the larger marble.

2 Players stand behind this line and take turns to shoot all six marbles, one by one, in the direction of the target marble.

3 You are allowed to hit other players' marbles as well as the larger target marble.

4 Count up the final score. A marble that gets close to the target is worth one point. If your other marbles are closer to the target than any or some of your opponents' marbles, you get one point for each of these as well.

5 The player with the highest score wins.

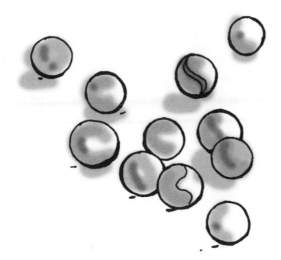

This miniature version of lawn bowling is good fo play inside on a rainy day. Remember to keep your hand steady as you shoot.

Hot Hands

 2   1   None

 Your reflexes must be real sharp. The player with the fastest reflexes (who can pull his or her hands away quickly from his or her opponent and avoid getting slapped) wins the match.

1 Face your opponent. Hold out your hands, palms up. He or she puts his or her hands on top of yours, palms down.

2 Try to slap his or her hands before he or she can pull them away.

3 Swap over once you have managed to touch the hands of the other player (even the smallest slap counts!)

4 Each hand slap is worth one point.

5 The first player to score three points is the winner.

The game is called hot hands because you have to pretend that your partner's hands are burning like red-hot coals and that you'll get burned if he or she touches you. You'll both get quite warm from all this hand slapping as well. Remember not to hit too hard! You don't want sore hands at the end of the game, do you?

12

Musical Chairs

 8 players, plus a leader   1   A chair for all but one of the players, CD player, CDs

---

 To see who is fastest in sitting down when the music stops.

1 Draw lots or toss up to choose a leader. This person is in charge of switching the music on and off. He or she is like a referee and watches what is going on to make sure no one cheats.

2 Before the music starts, stand in a circle facing sideways. (Players will not be able to see that there is one chair less than there are players.) For example, if four players are in the game there will only be three chairs to sit on.

3 When the music starts, circle round the chairs quickly. At no time can you touch a chair or you will be out.

4 When the music stops, quickly sit down on one of the chairs. Whoever stays standing on that turn is out.

5 The winner is the person who manages to sit on the one remaining chair when there are two players left.

13

Banana, Knife, and Fork

 6 or more 1 2 stools, a pair of dish washing gloves, a large banana, a coin, a napkin, a knife, a fork, a plate

 To try and eat as much of the banana as you can before the next player lays his or her hands on the napkin, cutlery, and gloves, and takes your place "at the table." If you finish the last slice, you have won!

1 Place the two stools side by side: the plate and the cutlery go on the first stool; the napkin and gloves on the second.

2 Players sit round the two stools in a circle. The youngest player is first to play.

3 When it is your turn, spin the coin in front of the other players. If you get "heads," do not budge. If you get "tails," rush over to the second stool, tie the napkin around your neck, pull on the gloves, and start to slice up the fruit (the only way to eat banana in this game.)

4 Remember, you cannot start eating unless the napkin is tied round your neck and the gloves are on, otherwise you lose your turn.

5 If another player comes up with "tails," he or she will rush over to you.

6 Players take turns to spin the coin as they try to get the person eating the banana off the stool.

7 Hand over the napkin and gloves. Tie the napkin around the neck of the other player. He or she must also pull on the gloves before beginning to eat.

8 As you are out, take up your place in the circle again.

9 The player who finishes the last slice of banana wins.

The Waiter

 5 to 15 2 Paper and pen

 The player who is the waiter has to remember his "customers" orders correctly while a lot of noise goes on in the background.

1 Draw lots or toss up to choose the waiter.

2 The other players sit at a table. While waiting for the waiter to take their orders, everyone pretends to have a noisy discussion with raised voices and lots of hand movements—all of this is designed to distract the waiter.

3 If you are chosen to be the waiter, come over to the table and ask each person for his or her order (including drinks.)

Listen hard and take in all this information without writing anything down.

4 You can take notes but only once all the orders have been placed or afterward to double-check the answers.

5 The game can be made more difficult by giving the waiter very detailed orders. For instance, "a BLT [bacon, lettuce, and tomato] sandwich with fries on the side," "a slice of cherry pie with lots of whipped cream," or "a bowl of spaghetti with grated melted cheese on top."

Human Chairs

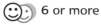

 6 or more   3   None

 To lean back and sit on the knees of the player right behind you to form a human chain. Lean too far back and everyone falls down. It is a real balancing act.

1 Stand in line and face in the same direction with your arms wrapped around each others' waists.

2 Remember: the first player in line is being hugged from behind while the last player in line only does the hugging.

Everyone else in between is being hugged as they do the hugging.

3 Now it is time for all six players to play the role of a chair. Gently bend your knees forward before slowly easing back onto the lap of whoever is immediately behind you! If you do not feel very stable in this position, try raising your heels off the floor as this can sometimes restore some extra balance.

Tchuka Ruma

 1   3   5 small bowls, 8 pebbles

 To collect all your counters in the "ruma" (the only empty bowl from your original setup.)

1 Place the five bowls in a line. Starting from the left and moving across to the far right, add two pebbles to each bowl.

2 Keep the bowl farthest to your right (the "ruma") empty.

3 Select one of the "filled" bowls and take out its contents.

4 Start to "sow" the pebbles (one by one) like seeds into the other bowls in a counterclockwise direction. Start from the left and move across to the right to distribute these pieces among the neighboring bowls.

5 If your last pebble ends up in the "ruma" bowl, you can move it from here by selecting the contents of a new bowl. If you have pebbles left over after "sowing" the "ruma," continue to distribute these pebbles into any adjacent bowls starting from the left.

6 If you place your last pebble in a bowl that is full, you must take out all the

pebbles and repeat the "sowing" process described in step three. If you end up placing the final pebble in an empty bowl that is not the "ruma," the game is over.

7 You win when all pebbles are collected in the "ruma" bowl.

Did you know that Tchuka Ruma is a traditional game of solitaire from Malaysia and the Philippines? It is played on a circular board with a ring of holes on it. One of the holes, the "ruma" (or home,) is larger than the others. At the beginning of the game, all holes, except the "ruma," are filled with an equal number of stones. The aim of the game is to collect as many stones in this empty hole as possible.

The Ice-Skating Rink

 2 or more, the help of an adult for hammering in the nails

 3

 A sturdy board (approx. 3 x 5 feet / 1 x 1.5 meters,) nails, a hammer, a thick glass bottle, sand, dish washing liquid, pencil

To complete the racing circuit by sending the bottle skidding between the nail tracks.

1 Use a pencil to sketch a racing circuit of two parallel lines (about 10 inches or 25 centimeters apart.) The borders of the track must be wide enough for the bottle to fit easily through them.

2 Ask an adult to hammer in the nails so they follow the shape of the parallel lines you have drawn. Nails should be hammered in halfway through the board with a gap of just over an inch (3 centimeters) between each one.

3 When the circuit is ready for racing, add a squirt of dish washing liquid to the surface of the board to help the base of the bottle glide along more easily.

4 Fill up half the bottle with sand to make it heavier and more stable.

5 Place the board on the floor and the bottle at the starting line.

6 Lift one end of the board and begin to gently tilt it this way and that so the bottle swerves as it moves down the circuit. Make sure it does not roll over.

7 If the bottle falls or rolls over at any time, it is the next player's turn and you have to go back to the beginning.

8 The player to reach the finishing line first wins.

Outside Games

King (or Queen!) of the Hill

 3 or more, plus an adult to supervise the game

 1

 None

To protect your territory from attack and not get knocked off your perch by the other players.

1 You can play this game anywhere, on any surface—grass, sand, or snow—but find an area where there is a hill, a mound, or a high point. Avoid playing in trees and from branches.

2 This game can get quite rough so please do not injure either yourself or your friends by unnecessary pushing and shoving—biting, kicking, and any other foul play is strictly not allowed!

3 Draw lots or toss up to see which player gets to be king or queen.

4 The king or queen climbs the hill to take his or her place at the top of the mound. The king or queen has to beat off any attackers who clamber up to try to pull, push, or shove him or her out of the way.

5 The attack continues from all sides until the king or queen has been forced off the hill.

6 The first player to scramble up to the hilltop and claim it is the next king or queen.

If you were a king or queen, you would defend your kingdom against an invading enemy, wouldn't you?

22

Red Light, Green Light

 4 or more   1   Stones, sticks, or chalk

 To tag the player who is the stoplight.

1 Draw lots or toss up to choose one player to be the stoplight.

2 If you are the stoplight, stand facing a tree or a wall.

3 The starting line is marked out on the ground in chalk (about 30 feet or 10 metres around away from you.)

4 The other players line up along this line in a row.

5 When you call out "green light!," all the players behind you must move forward as quickly as possible before you call out "red light!" and turn round. When you do, everyone must stop where they are. Whoever moves even a little must return to the starting line. The game continues with you calling out another "green light!" and so on.

6 The first person to reach you wins and becomes the stoplight in the next round.

This game teaches you the rules of traffic lights so it's very important to learn it well.

23

Hunter and Watchman

 4 or more   1   None

 If you are the hunter, to capture as many animals as possible. If you are an animal, not to get caught by the hunter or the watchman, and to free as many of the other animals as you can.

1 Draw lots or toss up to choose two players to be the hunter and the watchman.

2 The watchman stands in the middle of a circle clearly marked out with a border of stones. He or she cannot leave the circle until the game is over.

3 If you are an animal, start to run around the play area.

4 The hunter chases after you, trying to catch and bring back as many animals to the circle as he or she can.

5 The hunter leads any captured animals back to the watchman.

6 If you have been caught, you can be saved if one of the other animals who is still free touches you before you are taken into the circle. To do this, players must avoid stepping into the circle or touching another player once he or she is within the circle.

7 If you are tagged by the hunter or the watchman as you are trying to save one of the other animals, you are now captured and must go into the circle.

8 The game can be stopped at any moment.

Capture the Flag

 6 or more   1   2 rags, chalk for marking out game areas

 To steal the other team's flag without getting tagged.

1 Find a large play area.

2 Divide players into two teams, with an equal number on each side.

3 Draw lots or toss up to choose a leader for each team. Hand each leader their team flag.

4 Divide up the playing field so there is a middle area where members of both teams can run around chasing each other and two prisons (at either end) where members of the opposite team are held once they are tagged or captured. Your team's prison area doubles as your team's safety area.

5 Hide your team's flag. The opposite team does the same.

6 Both teams then break and run across the middle of the playing field trying to steal the opposite team's flag. You must make it back home without getting tagged. If you get tagged, you go to the other team's prison.

7 The only way to get out of jail is for one of your team members (who is not in prison) to touch you inside the area and free you. Be careful, however, because you can get recaptured if you are tagged on the opposite side of the field.

8 The first team to find the other group's flag and bring it to their side of the line wins the game.

This game involves a lot of running around so you might be out of breath by the end of it!

26

Hole in One

 2 or more   2   Plastic cup and coin (for each player)

 To aim your coin into the cup.

1. You and your opponent can play this game in your driveway or on the sidewalk outside your front door.

2. Lay the plastic cup on its side.

3. Sit or crouch on the ground (6 feet or around 2 metres away from the cup.)

4. Take turns to aim for the hole (cup) by rolling a coin toward it.

5. Each time the coin rolls in, you have scored a hole in one and one point.

6. The player with the highest score wins.

To score, keep your eye on the hole in the ground like a golf pro.

Beanbag Toss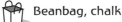

 2 or more   2   Beanbag, chalk

 To hit the marked sections of the target (especially the bull's-eye) with your beanbag.

1 Use chalk to draw the different sections of your target on the ground. Each section needs to be wide enough so that a tossed beanbag will fit easily without touching the borders. Check that the overall shape is roughly round.

2 Choose a point range from one to eight and mark each section with one point. The highest points should appear at or near the center and the lower points farther out.

3 Draw the throwing line (about 5 feet or 1.5 metres away from the target.)

4 Players take turns to toss the beanbag at the target—make sure you are standing behind the throwing line when you take aim.

5 Points are scored if the beanbag falls within a section but you get no points if it just touches one of the borders.

6 You can win in one of two ways: either by achieving the highest score or by being the first player to reach a maximum set score.

Why not divide your bull's-eye into "slices," like a pie or a dart board, to make it different from the norm?

29

Dodge Ball

 10 or more   2   A soft rubber ball, chalk

 To hit as many players from the rival team as you can and dodge their ball to avoid getting tagged.

1 Agree the size of the play area (33 x 13 feet / 10 x 4 metres is a good size.)

2 Mark it out in chalk.

3 Divide players into two teams so they face each other across the dividing line.

4 Each team sends one of their members to the opposing team's prison area. These two voluntary prisoners are placed here to get the game started. They will rejoin their team once a member of the opposing side gets hit and takes his or her place in prison.

5 During the game, players must stand within their respective boundaries.

Whoever has the ball tries to strike someone from the opposite team. If you score a hit, this person is sent to prison behind your team. If you are caught, you have to go to their prison but are allowed one more throw. From prison, you can catch any stray balls or block passes and try to hit rival players. If you do, you earn back your freedom and can return to your team.

6 Remember, the ball can never bounce before it touches a player—if it does, that person is tagged and must go to prison. If someone accidentally catches the ball, whoever threw the ball is out of the game.

7 Continue to play until all players from one team are in prison. The last player to go to prison gets three final tries to save himself.

Tug of War

 6 or more, plus an adult to supervise the game

 3

A rag, a long piece of strong rope

 To pull the opposite team over to your side, past the central line.

1. Divide up into two equal teams (in terms of size and strength.)

2. Tie the rag to the middle of the rope as a marker.

3. Draw or make a line on the ground. You can play this game on a soft surface like grass or sand.

4. Line up each team, one person behind the other, at either end of the rope. Leave about 5 feet (or 1.5 metres) of clear rope between the two teams.

5. Pick up the rope. The end player on either side acts as the anchor—it's best to choose the strongest member of your team for this role.

6. When both teams are in position, the supervising adult calls out "ready, get set, go!" and both sides start to pull in opposite directions. Use all your strength to try and drag the other team over to your side of the line.

7. If the first member of the other team crosses the line, your team wins.

This is a classic contest of strength, coordination, and teamwork. You have to work like two opposing forces of nature.

31

Triangular Tug of War

 3, plus an adult to supervise the game

 3

 A piece of rope or a clothesline, three handkerchiefs

 To be the first to grab your handkerchief off the ground.

1 Contestants should be of similar size and strength. Ask an adult to tie a piece of rope securely (10 feet or about 3 metres long) into a circle.

2 You and two other players pick up the rope. Pull it tight until it forms a triangle. All three of you should be facing outward so that you are holding the rope behind you.

3 The supervising adult places the handkerchiefs on the floor in front of each one of you.

4 You should always keep one hand on the rope. The first player to pick up the handkerchief with one hand is the winner!

This variation on tug of war can be played on a much smaller scale either in a small area or outside.

32

Races and Relays

Racing Bunnies

 8 to 30 (an even number), plus an adult to supervise the game

 1

Stones, chalk or sticks for marking outlines, whistle (optional)

To bounce your way to the finish line.

1. Using the chalk or the sticks and stones, mark out two lines on the ground (about 16 feet or 5 meters apart.) These will be your starting and turning lines.

2. Divide players into two equal teams with four or more players on each side.

3. Everyone lines up behind the starting line in single line. When everyone is ready, the supervising adult shouts "on your marks, get set, go!" or signals the start by blowing a whistle.

4. As the first player of your team, you must race toward the turning line hopping like a human bunny. To do this, bend your legs and lunge forward. When you get to the turning line, turn round and hop back toward the finish line. Your teammates can only set off once you (the first bunny) have completed the course and given the second bunny permission to race.

5. The first team to make it out and back is the bunny-hopping champions!

Who will be the happiest, "hoppiest" bunny around?

Three-Legged Race

4 or more
(an even number),
plus an adult to
supervise the game

2

A large scarf for every pair of players or some short pieces of rope, chalk for marking out starting and finish lines, whistle (optional)

 To be the first three-legged team (or pair of players) to cross the finish line.

1 Find a soft surface on which to play to avoid injuries. Mark the start and finish lines with chalk. They should be about 33–39 feet (or 10–12 meters) apart.

2 Divide the players into equal teams. Choose your partner and make sure you are both standing side by side. Bend down and securely tie his or her left leg to your right leg with the rope or scarf (bind together only the inside legs). Put your arm around your partner's shoulder. The other pairs of players do the same.

3 When everyone is ready, the two teams stand behind the start in two lines.

4 When the supervising adult calls out "on your marks, get set, go!" or signals the start by blowing a whistle, you and your partner (as the first couple from your team) run toward the finish line. Be prepared to take a few tumbles as you find your racing rhythm!

5 If you and your partner do fall over, just get straight back up and continue to race. Then turn round at the finish line and race back to tag the second couple in your team.

6 The first team to have its couples complete the race wins.

In this relay, choosing a partner the same height as you can really help keep you steady when you move together as one.

Twisted Arms Race

 2

8 to 20, plus an adult to supervise the game

A pile of about 50 small objects (buttons, bottlecaps, horse chestnuts, coins, etc.), whistle (optional)

 To complete a double pass down the team line in the fastest time possible. Use your right hand and pass from the front as you receive an object. Use your left hand and pass from the back as you return an object.

1. Divide the players into two equal teams. Choose a captain. All players sit down on the grass or the sidewalk.

2. Teammates sit in a line to the left of their leader and the two teams face each other.

3. Ask a supervising adult to place a pile of objects next to each leader.

4. When everyone is ready, the supervising adult says "on your marks, get set, go!" or signals the start by blowing a whistle. Each team captain starts to pass an object from down his or her end of the line, one at a time, to the player sitting down next to them. Objects can only be passed from the front using the right hand.

5. When an object reaches the opposite end of the line, the last player must now transfer the object to his or her left hand. Objects on their way back to the head of the line (and the captain) can only be passed from the back using the left hand.

6. The captain begins to make a small pile of returned objects.

7. Your team leader must be careful not to mix up new and returned objects in the same pile.

8. Continue passing objects in both directions until all have been returned to your captain.

9. The fastest team with the fewest mistakes is the winner.

The successful team will work like an automatic conveyor belt!

In this game, you have to concentrate on what you're doing. It's easy to forget which hand you need to use as you pass or receive the different objects.

Egg and Spoon Race

 5 or more, plus an adult to supervise the game

 2

A metal spoon and a hard-boiled egg (for each player,) whistle (optional)

 To race across the room balancing an egg on a spoon without dropping it.

1 Players line up against a wall holding a spoon by the handle. In the spoon is an egg. Everyone gets a little time to practice balancing their egg on their spoon before the race starts.

2 Ask an adult to place a chair about 6 feet (or just over 2 meters) away from the wall on the other side of the room.

3 When the supervising adult shouts the word "go" or signals the start by blowing a whistle, players race across the room, trying to keep the eggs balanced on their spoons. If your egg falls off, you cannot continue the race until it's back on the spoon. If it breaks, you're out of the game. Hopefully, there won't be any mess on the floor!

4 The first person to reach the chair, go around it from behind, and cross the finish line with their egg intact on their spoon is the winner. If teams are competing against each other, the first team to have all its players complete the course is the winner.

It's a good idea to have water and a towel handy to clean up any accidents. Be prepared to make some mess so remember to wear old clothes! Don't forget to ask an adult for permission if you're playing the game inside.

Races and relays don't necessarily have to be competitive with a winning and a losing team. Sometimes it's fun to just play and encourage everyone to take part.

Wheelbarrow Race

 4 or more (an even number), plus an adult to supervise the game

 3

stones or sticks for marking out lines, whistle (optional)

 To finish the race as a pair with one of you supporting the other by the legs as he or she crawls forward using only the arms.

1 On grass or soft sand, use a stone or a stick to mark out both the start and finish lines (30 feet or about 10 meters apart from each other.)

2 Divide everyone into pairs and choose your partner.

3 Pairs of players line up along the start line as they prepare to get into the human wheelbarrow position.

One player from each pair gets down on their hands and knees.

4 When the supervising adult calls out "on your marks, get set, go!" or signals the start by blowing a whistle, pick up your partner's legs. Hold them by the ankles at waist height as you try to "push" your partner (the human wheelbarrow) toward the finishing line.

5 Remember, broken wheelbarrows must be picked up where they collapsed—they cannot walk to the finish line!

6 The first pair to cross the finish line or the first team to have all its pairs complete the course is the winner.

You and your friends may end up with really dirty hands in this classic picnic race! Don't forget to wash up with soap and water after the race.

39

Piggyback Race

 4 or more (even number), plus an adult to supervise the game

  3

Stones or sticks for marking outlines, whistle (optional)

To carry your partner on your back, swap over, then race back to the finish line as a pair.

1. Find a place where there is grass or soft sand to avoid any injuries. Using a stone or a stick, mark out the starting and turning lines (they should be 30 feet or about 10 meters apart.)

2. For a proper race, divide everyone into pairs or teams of at least three pairs.

3. Place the players in position along the start line.

4. When the supervising adult calls out "on your marks, get set, go!" or signals the start by blowing a whistle, climb up onto your partner's back and loosely wrap your arms around his or her shoulders. Leave your legs dangling by their waist.

5. Your partner holds onto your legs and carries you piggyback as you both head toward the turning line. When he or she sets you down, you swap over. This time, you are the carrier and your partner the "piggy!"

6. Race back to the start line as a pair. If teams are playing, the second pair runs the course after the first pair have come back and so on.

7. The first to cross the finish line are the champions.

Children under age seven should not carry their friends piggyback as they have not yet got the strength or balance to do this. Older children may carry younger ones though.

40

Crab Relay

 8 to 30 (an even number), plus an adult to supervise the game

 3

 Stones, chalk, or sticks for marking outlines, whistle (optional)

 To crawl to the finish line making crab-like movements.

1 Using the chalk or the sticks and stones, mark out two lines on the ground (13–19 feet or about 4–6 meters apart.) These will be your start and turning lines.

2 Divide players into two equal teams with four or more players on each side.

3 When everyone is ready, the supervising adult shouts "on your marks, get set, go!" or signals the start by blowing a whistle.

4 As the first player of your team, you must scurry sideways toward the turning line (like a crab) and then come back to the start line.

5 The second player from your team can set off once you have returned and so on. The other players follow your example.

6 The winning crab crawlers are the team who first completes the race.

Picture how crabs scurry along the beach and you're halfway there!

41

Pass the Orange Race

 8 or more (an even number), plus an adult to supervise the game

 3

 2 firm oranges, whistle (optional)

Players must pass the fruit to their teammates using only either their feet or chin. Avoid dropping the orange on the ground or using your hands.

1 Divide players into two equal teams. Choose a captain for each side.

2 Everyone takes off their shoes and sits down on the floor in a line facing the opposite team.

3 The players' legs must be close together, side by side, and facing forward, with pointed toes.

4 When the supervising adult calls out "ready, get set, go" or signals the start by blowing a whistle, the first player (or captain) is given an orange to place on top of his or her feet.

5 The object of the game is to move the orange down the line to the next teammate who in turn balances the piece of fruit on his or her feet and moves it on. If you drop the orange before it reaches the feet of the next player, pick it up (using only your feet) and try to pass it on.

6 The first team to pass the orange down the line wins.

7 In a variation of the game, players stand side by side in line and pass the orange by tucking it under their chin and nuzzling it under the chin of the next player. The choice is yours!

How do you prefer to pass the orange? Using only your feet or tucking it under your chin and nuzzling it over to the next player?

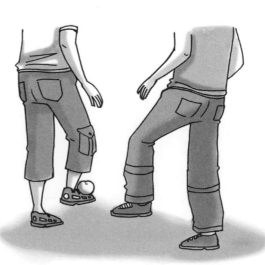

42

Hunts and
Hide-and-Seeks

Ghost in the Graveyard

 3 or more 1 None

 For the ghost to tag as many players as he or she can.

1. Find a big playing area at dusk with specific landmarks like a tree, fountain, porch, or a shed. These will serve as safe bases for players running away from the "ghost."

2. Choose a player to be the "ghost" or "it." The roles here are the opposite of those in *Classic Hide-and-Seek* on page 46. In this game, "it" hides while the other players stay at the base and count backwards from 50 to 0.

3. When the counting is over, players move away from the base looking for the missing ghost.

4. If you are picked to be the "ghost" or "it," do not wait to be found. Run around creeping up on the other players and try to tag as many of them by surprise as you can before they make it back to the base.

5. If the roles are reversed, for example, and *you* spot the ghost coming, warn the other players.

6. Tagged players are out until the end of the round when there is no one left to tag or players have safely reached the base.

7. At the end of every round, those players who are still safe count backwards again.

8. Players who have already been tagged become ghosts, and team up with you (if you are the ghost) to chase down the remaining players until there is only one person left.

9. The last player "alive" wins.

This classic run and chase game includes elements of tag and hide-and-seek so parts of it may sound very familiar to you.

Classic Hide-and-Seek

 3 or more 1 None

 To find and tag as many players as possible before they reach home base.

1 Agree on the boundaries of the hiding area and the location of the home base (this could be a step or a porch) with the other players.

2 Draw lots or toss up to decide who will be the seeker or "it." This person will have to search for all the other players once they have gone into hiding.

3 If you are "it," close your eyes and slowly count to 50 or 100 while the remaining players rush to find good hiding places.

4 When you have finished counting, call out "ready or not, here I come," and go looking for the hidden players. Players can come out of hiding and run for the safety of home base when you are looking in the wrong direction or are momentarily distracted.

5 If you stick so close to the home base that no other player is able to make it back without you tagging them, a "zone" can be set around it where no player is allowed to hide. In this way, you will be forced to hunt farther out.

6 Any players you find or tag are out of the game until the next round when a new "it" is chosen.

7 Continue the game until everyone is either caught or home free. The first person you tagged is "it" in the next round.

Champion hide-and-seek players are good at choosing their cover and timing their escape, and are full of surprises when they are "it!"

Sardines

 3 or more   1   None

 To find the person who is hiding and hide with them.

1 All players (except one) close their eyes. This person runs and hides while the others count to 50.

2 You need a house large enough to have plenty of good places to hide in (for example behind a door or a curtain, under the bed, inside the shower cubicle, inside a cupboard, and so on.)

3 When the counting is over, a second player goes in search of the first who is now hiding away somewhere in the house. If he or she finds the original player, he or she can join this person in their hiding place. If not, that particular seeker is out of the game.

4 The game continues until all players have had the chance to seek.

5 Those players still hiding, packed into small spaces like sardines, are the winners.

This wriggly game lets you join your buddies in small, tight spaces where there isn't much room to move around. Try not to give yourself away by laughing!

Cops and Robbers

 6 or more (even number)   □ 1   None, coin (optional)

If you are a cop, to catch as many criminals as you can. If you are a robber, to avoid getting stopped and caught by the police!

1 Divide the players into two equal teams. Toss up or draw lots to decide who wants to play the cops in the first round.

2 Select a team base that doubles as a "jail." This could be a porch or a stoop.

3 The cops gather round the home base and count to 50 while the robbers go and hide.

4 When the counting is finished, the cops begin to chase and tag any robbers they touch.

5 Criminals who are caught are automatically led back to jail. A jail break can be staged by a member of the robbers team if he or she can tag the jail

and free all the prisoners inside without being tagged by a cop.

6 The freed prisoners sit out the rest of the game until all the free robbers have been stopped by the cops.

7 At the end of the first round, count the number of robbers remaining in jail. Are there many prisoners (because there was no successful jail break) or just one or two?

8 Teams then swap and the new cops round up the new robbers. At the end of the second round, count the number of prisoners in jail.

9 The team that catches the largest number of criminals when it is their turn to play the cops wins the game.

Good guys and bad guys battle it out in this classic, action-packed, hide-seek-and-chase game.

Let your imagination run wild when deciding what to call the teams. They could be heroes and villains, cops and robbers, angels and devils, good guys and bad guys, aliens and humans, knights and dragons, or hunters and lions—to give you a few examples!

Mice and Wolves

  15 or more, plus an adult or older child to supervise the game

2

Paper, pencils, felt-tips, sticky tape

 Depending on which drawing is pinned to your back, your task is to avoid being "eaten" by those animals who can hunt you and tag the ones who fear you.

1 The supervising adult sets a time limit for the game and divides players into five teams—mice, cats, dogs, wolves, and hunters—and prepares different animal head drawings for each of the teams. Each player is taken to one side and a piece of paper with a drawing is taped to their back before the game begins.

2 To have a good game, group size should be organized so you begin with the largest group and end with the smallest. This means the order should be: mice, cats, dogs, wolves, and finally only one or two hunters (no more.)

3 Players spread out across the whole play area and try to go and hide. If you bump into another player, quickly check to see who you are up against. Depending on the animal or animals, you will either run away or give chase. Be ready for a lightning-fast game as the roles suddenly change and the hunter becomes the hunted (or the other way round.)

4 There are rules to follow: mice can be hunted by everyone except the hunters. Cats can be hunted by dogs and wolves but not by hunters. Dogs chase mice and cats but need to avoid wolves. The wolf can track everyone down but flees from the hunter. If two wolves join forces, they can hunt a hunter.

5 When someone touches you, you both must go to the supervising adult. He or

A run-or-chase game full of twists and turns, where players either flee from one another or start to run after each other in hot pursuit!

50

she will place the weaker animal into the stronger group. So, for example, if someone has tagged you (and they are a cat and you are a mouse,) you automatically become a cat. This is a general rule of thumb for all animals except two: any animals tagged by the hunter and any hunters touched by two wolves turn into mice.

6 For a fair game at all times, ask the supervisor to keep numbers between animal populations as well-balanced as possible.

7 The game ends when the time limit runs out.

The Great Duel

 8 or more, plus an adult or older child to supervise the game

 2

Clothes pins, sticks of chalk, handkerchief (for each player), whistle (optional)

 To collect as many weapons as possible from the rival team.

1. Find and mark out a very large play area like the park or the woods.

2. Divide the players into two teams and give each participant three weapons: a clothes pin, a stick of chalk, and a handkerchief.

3. At the signal to start, players scatter around this area. When you find a player from the opposite team, you both must cry out "challenge!" If you beat your opponent to the battle cry, you decide on which weapon to use for the following duel.

4. If you choose the chalk, the winner must be first to scribble on their opponent's shoe. If you succeed, the other player must hand over his or her stick of chalk.

5. If you choose the clothes pin, the winner must be the first to pin it to their opponent's clothes. If you succeed, the other player must hand over his or her clothes pin.

6 If you choose the handkerchief, both of you must tuck yours into the back pocket of your pants so that it hangs from behind like a tail. If you succeed in snatching your opponent's handkerchief, he or she must hand it over to you.

7 If one player challenges another with a weapon that he or she has lost, there is no duel.

8 You're out of the game if you lose any of your weapons.

9 After a time, players gather round and the supervising adult starts to stack up the three objects (chalk, pins, and handkerchiefs) to count up how many of each weapon were taken by each team.

10 The team with the largest number of stolen weapons wins.

This large-scale chasing game is three games rolled into one—tag, a version of paper/scissors/stone, and hide-and-seek. It'll really put you through your paces!

Scavenger Hunt

 2 or more, plus an adult to supervise the game

 3

 A piece of paper and a plastic or paper sack for each player; a pencil; timer; a collection of small items (a piece of gum, keyring, photograph, spinning top, toothbrush) as objects to hide around the house

Players race against each other to hunt down all of the objects on the list within a set time limit.

1 This version of the hunt is designed to be played indoors by single players.

2 Ask an adult to prepare a list of items that can be easily found around the house.

3 These things should be everyday objects (see below). For younger kids, the list can be very specific while for older players clues can be more open to interpretation. For example, the list could say: "Find something that goes inside your mouth." This could be a toothbrush, a toothpick, or dental floss, for instance.

4 At the signal, everyone is given a copy of the list and a sack for collecting any objects found.

5 Players go off around the house in search of booty.

6 The first player able to cross everything (or most items) off the list within the time limit is the winner. To make the game more competitive, this hunt can also be played in teams.

Players can get very wrapped up in this game right to the end, as they continue to tick items from the list.

Party Games

Statues

 4 or more, plus an adult to supervise the game　　 1　　 None

 To stand as still as you can when the sculptor calls out "statues!"

1 Gather round in a group in a room or backyard—somewhere where all players can move about freely without breaking anything!

2 Draw lots or toss up to decide who will be "it" or the "sculptor."

3 If you are the sculptor, take a player by the wrist and spin them round three times before letting go.

4 As soon as you've released this player, he or she must strike a pose and hold it for a period of time. He or she is now a statue. Players have to stay frozen in these positions for as long as they can without even moving an eyebrow.

5 Spin the other players, one by one, so they can also assume statue poses.

6 Now that everyone is a statue, go around inspecting every player, trying to catch out anyone who's moving (even if just slightly) or trying to make them giggle so they lose their concentration. Making faces, silly noises, and even tickling is allowed but no hitting please!

7 If you're a statue and move even the tinniest fraction, you're out of the game.

8 The last statue to remain standing perfectly still is the winner and becomes the sculptor in the next round.

The Gods

 3 or more, plus an adult to be the DJ   1   A hardback book for each player, a CD player, or radio

---

 To move from one end of the room to the other in time to the music (as it switches on and off) without dropping the book on your head.

1 Find a space either inside or outside with plenty of room in which to move around. Players take all their cues from the music so you have to listen very carefully. Ask an adult or older child to operate the music, switching it on and off as often as the game requires. This game is like a more relaxed version of *Musical Chairs* (see page 13.)

2 Hand each player a hardback book of similar size and weight. If someone is a little older or a little stronger, he or she should be given a book that is slightly heavier than the others.

3 Players spread out round the room. Place the book on your head. Remember, you can extend your arms for added balance.

4 When the music starts (slow and soft is best), this is your signal to begin walking round the room, stepping forward slowly and gently so the book does not topple from your head. Continue to move, so long as there is music playing in the background.

5 When the music stops, all the players must also stop and slowly go down on one knee. Hold this position until the music restarts, then slowly come back up again and carry on gliding forward. (This is harder than it sounds and concentration is a must!)

6 If the book happens to slide off your head, you're out of the game, regardless of whether you were walking or kneeling at the time.

7 The player who can keep the book on his or her head the longest is the book-balancing champion. Congratulations!

Stand tall and hold your head up high as if you were a Greek god or goddess.

58

Pass the Parcel

 4 or more, plus an adult or older child to be the starter and parcel-wrapper

 1

A small toy or candy, wrapping paper, scissors, tape, a music source that can be easily switched on and off

 To be the first player to unwrap the last layer of the gift when the music stops.

1 Ask an adult to prepare a mystery present wrapped up in at least ten layers of wrapping paper. The brighter the colors and the crazier the designs of the papers the better!

2 The players sit round in a circle on the floor.

3 An adult or older child switches the music on and players begin to pass the parcel in a clockwise direction.

4 Continue to move the present around from hand to hand until the music suddenly stops. If you are left holding the parcel, unwrap one of the layers and discard the extra paper.

5 The music comes on again and the passing restarts. It is important to keep a cool head in this game as the layers come off one by one as the music stops and starts—it can get nerve-racking!

6 The player lucky enough to tear off the final piece of wrapping when the music stops keeps the prize.

Be the first person to put their hands on the last layer of the parcel – that way, you keep the surprise that's inside!

Blowing Bubbles

 4 or more (an even number)   2   A dish washing liquid or bubble solution, a bubble wand (for each player), a stick of chalk

 To blow a bubble and work together as a team to move it across the field, past the opposite team's goal line.

1 Set up the play area. Mark three parallel lines 8 feet (or 2.5 meters) long with a space of 37 inches (or about 95 centimeters) between each line.

2 Give each player a bottle of bubble solution and a wand.

3 Divide the players into two teams. They stand facing each other on either side of the middle line. The goal line is the line behind each team.

4 The game starts with one player from each team blowing a bubble. As the bubbles rise, the two teams take turns to blow furiously on theirs to send it across the middle line and over the heads of the opposite team into their territory. Your aim is to get your team's bubble past the opposite goal line.

5 You cannot touch the bubble with any part of your body (including your nose or forehead) but, other than that, anything goes! Do make sure, however, that your bubble does not burst before it has made its way across the field!

6 Players can cross the central line and chase the opposite team's bubble to move it away from their own goal line.

7 Your team gets one point if it moves the bubble over the goal line of the other team.

8 If the bubble pops before a goal is scored, the two teams line up again and start a new round. Teams take turns to blow the bubbles.

9 The team with the most points wins the match.

Pin the Tail on the Donkey

 4 or more, plus adults to set up the game and spin the blindfolded players

 2

A large sheet of cardboard, a paper tail for each player, sticky tape or thumbtacks, paint, felt-tips, a blindfold, scissors

To pin the tail on the donkey correctly while blindfolded.

1. Choose a playing area with plenty of room to move around in.

2. Ask an adult to help you draw a large picture of a donkey on the sheet of cardboard. Hang it up on a wall at eye level.

3. Cut out as many donkey tail strips as there are players. Insert a pin or thumbtack near one end of each tail otherwise they will not stay on (or use sticky tape instead.)

4. Each player writes his or her initials on the tail they are given.

5. Remember, the donkey needs to be facing you from the side. If you want to use other animals, like a lion or an elephant, these will also work well with this game.

6. Each player is blindfolded, one at a time, and spun around three times (make sure you don't get dizzy and fall over!) and pointed in the direction of the drawing.

7. Come forwards, toward the wall, and stick the tail as close to the place where a real donkey's tail would be.

8. The player who comes closest to pinning the tail in the right place on the donkey is the winner.

Try to use your memory to picture the donkey in your head!

Simon Says

 3 or more 3 None

 To copy the actions of the player who is Simon without messing up! He or she, in turn, must say "Simon says..." every time an instruction is given to the other players.

1 Draw lots or toss up to choose a player to be Simon.

2 The other players stand in a line facing this person.

3 If you are Simon, at the signal to start give the group instructions they can follow. Remember to *always* start any command with the words "Simon says..." For example, "Simon says, clap your hands!" or "Simon says, jump up and down!" Everyone copies your movements and tries not to make any mistakes until you give players a new set of instructions. (Players need to watch out for a fast-talking Simon: this kind of player can really steer the game to his or her advantage!)

4 To clinch the game, players must try to avoid being caught out as you watch their every move like a hawk. Remember, players don't *have* to follow a command unless you say "Simon says" first. This is the bit of the game that confuses a lot of people and, if you are a quick-thinking Simon, you will use this trick to get players out.

5 Players drop out one by one until there is one person left in the game.

6 This person is Simon in the next round.

Did you know that this game began as an army drill?

Limbo Dancing

 4 or more   3   A long stick, broom handle or a curtain rod

 To clear the stick or rod from underneath by twisting or bending backward but without losing your balance or touching it with any part of your body.

1 Two players hold up the stick at chest height at either end.

2 The other players line up behind each other and try to shimmy under the stick, but without touching it at any time.

3 Shuffle your feet forward as you try to shimmy backward with your arms held out for balance. Your head must be the last part of your body to go under the stick. This can be really difficult!

4 When everyone has had their turn, lower the stick a notch. Then the twisting can begin again but with gradually less room to move around in. Going under the stick without making any body contact becomes harder and harder.

5 You're out if you bump your head, lose your balance, or touch the stick. See if you can hold out the longest!

6 The last player to be out is the champion limbo dancer.

7 You can also play this game to music (which might help you to coordinate your body movements better.)

Originally a dance from the West Indies, this game puts your bendy abilities and concentration to the test!

Guessing Games

I Spy

 2 or more 1 None

 To identify as many objects as you can by their color or initial letters.

1 Sit together in a room inside or outside in a backyard.

2 Choose an object that everyone can see and say: "I spy, with my little eye, something that is _____." Fill in the blank with a color. Or, if you were looking at a clock, you would say: "I spy, with my little eye, something with HANDS."

3 Whoever guesses right is the winner.

4 To make the game more challenging, remember to choose something that shares a color with other objects around you to keep your friends from guessing too easily (many things are brown for example—trees, dogs, nuts, and so on.)

5 Make the game even harder by using the first letter of an object's name as a clue. For example, if you choose your dog, you can say: "I spy, with my little eye, something beginning with D."

6 The best version of the game is to give each player a letter and they must each then pick something beginning with that letter. If you are given the letter C, you could say words like caterpillar, cat, chair, and so on.

This game can be a fun way of practicing the letters of the alphabet.

What Am I Touching?

  2 to 15   1   Objects with different textures (wet sand, chestnuts, semolina, ice, fruits, vegetables, etc.)

 To guess the objects you are given to touch.

1 Choose a group of objects from around the house that are different shapes and sizes. Make sure they feel quite different from one another—some can be smooth, others rough; some cold, others warm, and so on.

2 Players take turns to be blindfolded. When it's your turn, you must guess the identity of the object or substance only by touch. Players can also put their hands behind their back when being handed objects. Good luck—see how many you get right!

3 Whoever gets the most correct guesses wins.

4 You can also play this game in teams.

Pictionary

 4 or more   2   A sheet of paper and a pencil

 One player does a drawing of a word picked by the opposite team. His or her teammates have to guess the word within a given time limit.

1. Divide the players into two teams, with the same number of players on each side.

2. Draw lots or toss up to see who goes first.

3. The team who wins chooses a word for the other team to guess.

4. The team who loses picks one of its players to be the artist.

5. As the artist, you're responsible for making a sketch of the word suggested by the opposite team. Your teammates will have to guess the word and you cannot give them *any* clues.

6. Someone from the first team comes over and whispers the word in your ear.

7. Once you've understood what the word is, start to draw the object. During this time, you cannot speak, gesture, or make noises. However, your teammates can make as many guesses and make as much noise as they want.

8. If your team guesses the word correctly before the time runs out, they score one point. (A team has one minute to try to come up with the correct answer.) You and your team choose a word for the opposing team to guess the next time.

9. If your team guesses the word incorrectly or after the minute is up, the first team wins and they get to choose another word to be drawn.

Ready? Set? Draw! You do not need to be an artist to be good at this great draw and guess game. It is the originality of your sketch that makes it fun (and often gives away good clues, too.)

Rhyming Charades

 4 or more   2   Pencil and paper for keeping score

 Having been given a rhyming word as a clue, discover the mystery word by using mime to check your guesses with the audience.

1 Divide the players into two teams. Team one is the actors and team two is the audience.

2 Team one leaves the room while team two decides on the word to be acted out by team one.

3 Once this is chosen, team two chooses a word that rhymes with the mystery word. This word must be given to team one as a clue.

4 The more rhymes the mystery word has the better.

5 Team two returns to the room and is given the rhyming word as a clue.

6 It must now use mime to check their guesses with the audience. For example, if the mystery word is "took," players may want to act out "cook" or "hook" in front of the audience by pretending to whisk eggs or go fishing. If the acting is good, the audience will call out "No, it's not cook!" or "No, it's not hook!" and so on.

7 Actors are allowed up to three guesses. If team one guesses correctly before all three attempts are up, the point goes to them. After that, the point is awarded to the audience team for having beaten the team of actors.

8 Teams swap over at the end of the first round. Then the new audience team chooses a word.

9 Teams swap over yet again at the end of the second round.

10 Teams carry on alternating roles until one team scores 10 points and is declared the winner.

The key to this game is choosing a word with lots of different rhymes so your opponents get confused and make several wrong guesses.

Who Am I?

 4 or more   2 Headbands, sticky labels, felt-tips

 To guess the name of the person written on your headband.

1 Players sit in a circle and are given headbands to tie round their heads.

2 Every player also receives a blank, sticky label. Write down the name of a famous person on the label and stick it on the headband of the player opposite you.

Be careful no one sees you writing this name down because that would give the game away!

3 When everyone else has finished doing the same and is ready to play, players start to ask each other questions about the name on their foreheads.

4 The first player to figure out who they are is the winner.

What's that Tune?

 3 or more 3 None

 To guess the name of a tune after hearing only a few notes.

1 Choose a player to be the hummer or singer. If you are this person, start the game by humming or whistling the first note of a well-known song.

2 The other players try to guess the name of the song from that single note. Players take turns trying to guess the famous tune. You'll soon find out how hard this is to do!

3 Now repeat the beginning of the tune, adding one note each time until someone finally figures out the name of the song.

4 This person becomes the singer in the next round.

Music fans with a good ear will love this memorable musical guessing game.

Murder in the Dark

 10 or more   3   Playing cards

 A killer is hiding among the players! The detective must unmask him or her by staging an interrogation and asking questions.

1 Gather all the players in a room, preferably one lit by a single light.

2 Take out the same number of cards from the deck as there are players. Make sure you include the King of Diamonds and Jack of Spades.

3 Each player chooses a card and looks at it before putting it away in his or her pocket without letting anyone see it. Whoever chooses the King of Diamonds is the detective. Whoever chooses the Jack of Spades is the killer.

4 The light is switched off and players start to move about in the shadows.

5 If you are the detective, stand by the light switch, ready to turn it back on.

6 In the dark, whoever is the killer chooses his or her victim by putting both hands on this player's shoulders. This person lets out a scream and falls down to the ground. Don't be frightened—no one gets really hurt as it's all pretend!

7 After 10 seconds, switch the light back on.

8 As the detective, this is your chance to take action—show everyone your card and start to interrogate the other players. It's best to question them as a group rather than one by one. Ask lots of questions about their whereabouts and alibis (like where they were last, where they have been since, who they were with, etc.)

9 The detective has four chances to discover the identity of the killer. If all four guesses are wrong, you are out of the game. If you unmask your villain, you can consider yourself the pride of the police department!

10 Players who are wrongly accused can show their cards to prove their innocence.

Hand Games

Origami Challenge

  1   1   Paper, pencil or pen, scissors, and colored crayons

 To make a fully working 3-D object from a flat sheet of paper!

1 To make a triangle from a rectangular sheet of paper, make a diagonal fold from the bottom left corner.

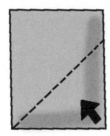

2 Using the scissors, cut off the rectangle at the top.

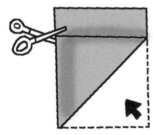

3 Fold over the two opposite ends of the triangle to form a smaller triangle.

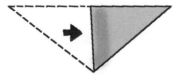

4 Open up the paper, uncreasing all the folds.

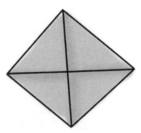

5 Fold one corner into the center. Repeat with the opposite corner.

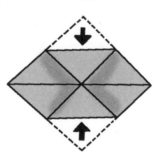

6 Repeat with the other two corners so you have a square.

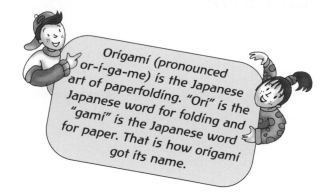

Origami (pronounced or-i-ga-me) is the Japanese art of paperfolding. "Ori" is the Japanese word for folding and "gami" is the Japanese word for paper. That is how origami got its name.

7 Flip the paper over. Fold a corner over the center. Repeat with the opposite corner.

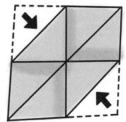

8 Fold over the two last corners so you have a smaller square.

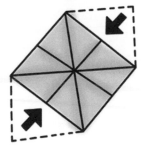

9 Fold the square in half. Unfold and then fold in half the other way.

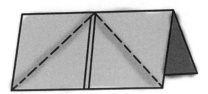

10 Unfold and pull the four ends together, making a diamond-like shape. Shade each of the square flaps a different color with the crayons. Pick up each of the flaps and put your fingers inside. Move the four parts around.

This type of mental activity encourages you to "see" the shape in your head before you fold over the flat surface of the paper and turn it into a three-dimensional object. This skill takes a bit of practice but is very useful for other games as well.

Paper, Scissors, Stone

 2 or more   1   None

 To defeat your opponent's weapon of choice using one of three hand gestures (paper, scissors, or stone.)

1 Stand or sit facing your opponent with one hand behind your back.

2 Count 1, 2, 3, then thrust your hidden hand into the center and quickly make one of three simple hand signs: a closed fist (rock,) a flat, open hand, palm-down, with all the fingers extended (paper,) or a hand with forefinger and middle finger extended and separated into a "v" shape (scissors.)

3 The match is won according to these rules:

* The paper covers the stone (the paper wins.)

* The scissors cut the paper (the scissors win.)

* The stone smashes or blunts the scissors (the stone wins.)

4 If you both choose the same weapon, it's a tie and you both have another go.

5 The game is usually ends after five goes with the best score as the winner.

80

The Well

 5 or more 2 None

 To match the nouns called out with the correct hand and body gestures.

1 Stand in a circle outside or in the backyard. Draw lots or toss up to choose the leader.

2 Before you start, you must select objects you want to use in the game and give them each a sign. For example, touching your head or any other part of the body.

3 All players close their right hand into a loose fist. This is your "well." Leave a gap in the middle (so the fingers of other players can fit in here.)

4 The leader starts by calling out the names of the different objects and players acknowledge these objects with their free hand using the chosen signs.

5 When the leader calls out "my well," everyone inserts their left forefinger into the gap of their right fist.

6 When the leader calls out "my neighbor's well," players put their left and right forefinger into the wells of the players on either side.

7 Anyone who plays the leader will try to catch you out when delivering his or her instructions so that the movement you make doesn't match what is called out. You have been warned!

To sharpen your concentration skills and to avoid a mistake, try not to look at the leader but focus on what he or she is saying.

String Challenge 1: The Bowl on a Plate

 1   2   Just over 3 feet (or 1 meter) of nylon elastic string tied at the ends works best but normal string is also fine

---

 To pull a single piece of string into various loops that together look like a "bowl on a plate."

1 Slip the length of string in front of the fourth, middle, and second finger of each hand. Gently stretch the length of string on either side.

2 Slip your forefingers through the opposite side of the string. Start with your right hand and repeat with your left.

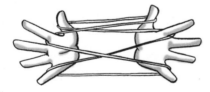

3 Slip both thumbs under the third loop (start with the loop closest to you.)

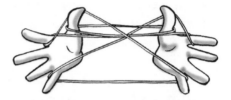

4 Slide both thumbs under the first loop.

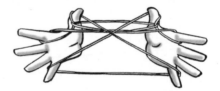

5 Release the string from your little fingers to achieve the "bowl on a plate" effect.

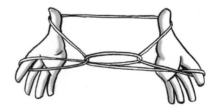

 Many shapes and patterns known as figures can be made from a loop of string held between the hands.

String Challenge 2: The Eiffel Tower

 1   2   Just over 3 feet (or 1 meter) of nylon elastic string tied at the ends works best but normal string is also fine

 To go from a "bowl on a plate" shape to the Eiffel Tower in a single move.

1 To go from one pattern to the next, catch the uppermost part of the first loop in your mouth.

2 Release both thumbs and pull down, holding the string firmly through your teeth.

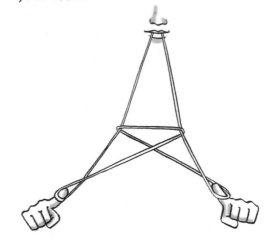

You need nimble fingers to play string games or your figures can literally tie you up in knots!

83

String Challenge 3: Dreamcatcher

 1 3 Just over 3 feet (or 1 meter) of nylon elastic string tied at the ends works best but normal string is also fine

 To create a woven pattern typical of Native American string art.

1 Repeat steps one and two from the Bowl on a Plate (see page 82.) Release the thumbs.

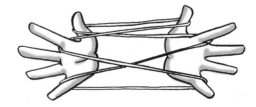

2 With your thumbs, grab the last strand from underneath and pull it toward you. Your thumbs must both be inside the loop.

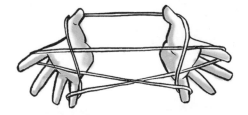

3 Move your thumbs over the second string to find the third loop. Release your pinkies.

4 With your pinkies, go over the fourth string and catch the third.

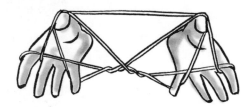

5 Release your thumbs. Move them over the first two strands so you can trap the third.

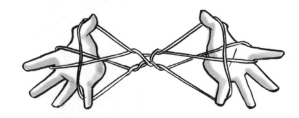

6 Slide your thumbs inside both forefinger loops.

7 Insert your thumbs between the first and the second strand.

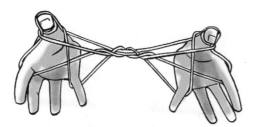

8 Insert your forefingers inside the first triangular gaps below your thumbs.

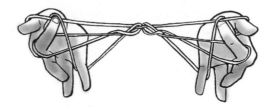

9 Release your pinkies. With a twisting motion of your hand, you now have a dreamcatcher.

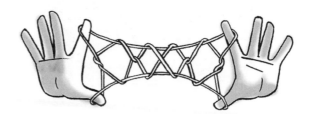

Each string figure has a name. Sometimes songs are sung and stories told as the figures are being made. In Native American culture, dreamcatchers help a person sleep well by keeping bad dreams away.

String Challenge 4: The Parachute, Dad's Pants, Mom's Apron, Grandma's Shoes

 1 3 Just over 3 feet (or 1 meter) of nylon elastic string tied at the ends works best but normal string is also fine

 To go from one figure to the next in a series of amazing string shapes. The other three figures are continuations of The Parachute.

1 Repeat steps one and two from the Bowl on a Plate on one hand (see page 82.)

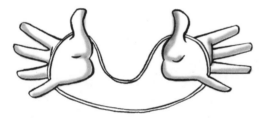

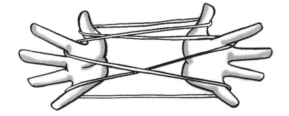

2 With your other hand, pull the middle string then release it.

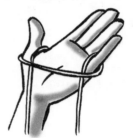

3 Pull the middle string again.

4 Move the string to the other side of your hand.

5 With your free hand, pull the thumb and pinkie loops.

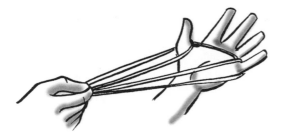

6 Move these two loops to the other side of your hand as you place one finger in between each strand.

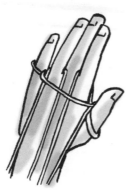

7 Slide these four strands under the string which is at the top of your hand.

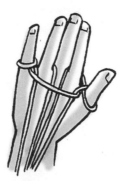

8 Move the string over to the other side of your hand and pull it toward you. You've just opened your parachute!

These next few figures are quite challenging, so practice hard until they become easier. When you can do them, why not try and tell your friends a story as you make each of the different figures?

9 Release the bottom of your parachute. With your other hand, catch the loops behind your forefinger and fourth finger, and pull them over these fingers. Pull down.

dad's pants. Pull down. You have just created an apron for mom!

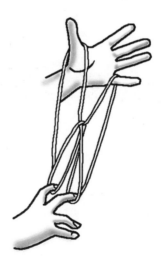

12 Release your pinkie to make shoes for grandma!

10 You've just made pants with large pockets for dad!

11 Release the bottom of dad's pants. Place the forefinger and middle finger of your other hand inside the two pockets of

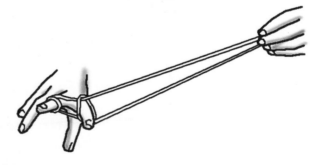

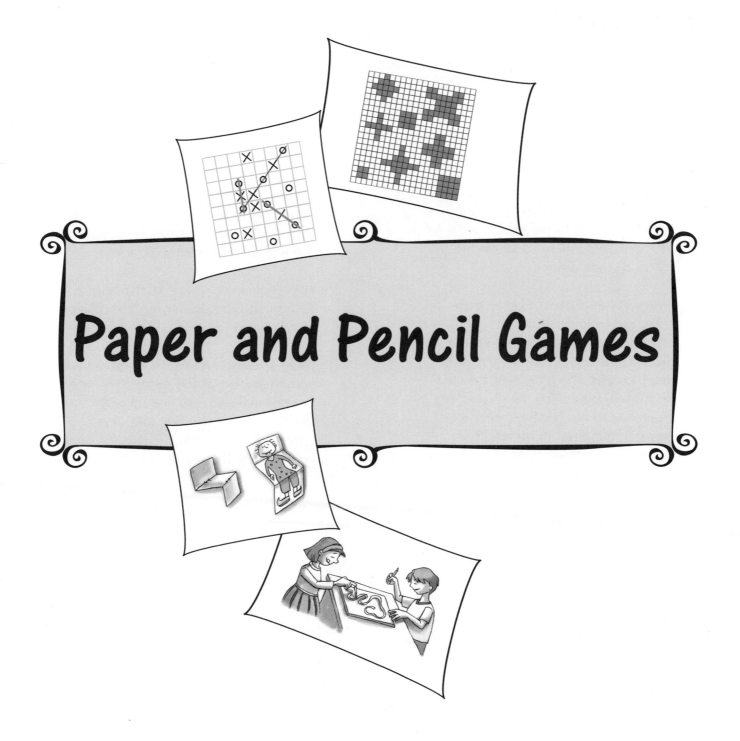

Paper and Pencil Games

Little Monster

 3 1 Paper, pencils, and color pencils or crayons (optional)

 Players can have fun creating a really odd-looking character by drawing sections of the figure separately without being allowed to see the parts already drawn.

1 You will need a rectangular piece of paper (8 inches long or roughly 20 centimeters.) Fold it into three sections. Draw two small lines over each crease. The lines over the first fold show how wide the character's neck has to be. The lines over the second fold point to the width of the character's waistline.

2 Draw a head in the first section of the paper. Make sure your character's neck fits within or is the same thickness as the two marks over the first fold.

3 Fold your section over so the head is hidden and then hand the folded paper to the second player.

4 He or she now draws the body in the second section of the paper. The neck line here should also line up with the marks over the first fold. The character's waist must match the gap between the lines over the second fold.

This great game is non-competitive and really creative. It will get your imagination going and let everyone join in (with hilarious results.)

90

5 The third player draws the figure from the waist down to the feet.

6 Fold out the sheet of paper to view the amazing "monster" you have created. Does anyone around you have a straight face?

Follow that Line!

 2   1   2 pencils, a sheet of paper

 To be the first person to cross the finish line.

1 Each player is given a pencil.

2 Copy the racetrack as shown in the picture below. The track should be about about half an inch (or 1 centimeter) wide. Mark the start line and the finish line.

3 Each player takes a turn to place his or her pencil on the starting line. Hold it in a vertical position with the tip of your finger, then push the pencil down into the paper and gently try to flick it across so it begins to draw a line before bouncing off the surface of the paper.

4 At the next turn, each player sets out from the point at which their line left the racetrack on the previous go.

5 The first person to complete the track wins the match.

OXO

 2   2   A sheet of graph paper, 2 different color pencils, a ruler

 To spot and strike through as many OXO series inside the grid as possible.

1 Using the pencil and ruler, draw an 8 x 8 playing grid on graph paper.

2 Choose who will be Xs and who will be Os. Xs go first. Each player is given a pencil to write their symbol.

3 Take turns to fill in one square at a time with either an X or an O.

4 Strike through any OXO sequence—vertically, horizontally, or diagonally—on the line intersections and close it off from your opponent.

5 Every completed series is worth one point.

6 Whoever has the most points once all the spaces on the grid are full, wins.

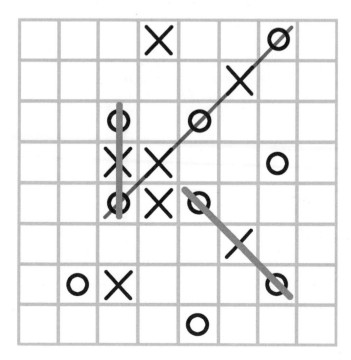

This game of tick-tack-toe "on the lines" can be mastered in a matter of minutes.

Tick-Tack-Toe with Numbers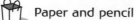

 2   3   Paper and pencil

 To be the first player to complete a line of numbers that add up to 15.

1 Draw a standard nine-square grid on the piece of paper with two parallel vertical lines crossed by two parallel horizontal lines.

2 Your opponent's numbers are the four even numbers between 1 and 9 (2, 4, 6, and 8.)

3 Your numbers are the five odd numbers between 1 and 9 (1, 3, 5, 7, and 9.)

4 You go first because you have one more digit to your name. Write down an odd number in any of the squares on the grid.

5 Your opponent does the same and writes down an even number.

6 Race each other to claim any rows of numbers that add up to 15 either in a vertical, horizontal, or diagonal line.

7 The game is won by whoever completes the first line or the most lines.

8 The game can be tied if all the squares have already been filled.

9 Swap over being odds and evens for the next round of the game.

This game puts the bite back into the old game of noughts and crosses. This version is for older children.

Growing Crystals

 2 or more   3   A sheet of graph paper, a pencil, and a different color crayon for each player

 To "grow" crystal shapes inside the grid by filling in squares and developing symmetrical patterns.

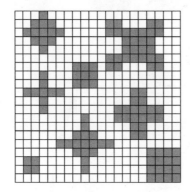

1 Mark off a grid (20 squares by 20 squares) on the sheet of graph paper. If there are more than two players, the grid should be larger (increased by about 10 squares for every additional player.)

2 Try to see the shape of your crystal in your head first. It can be a thick or a thin cross, a small or a large square, or a diamond-like shape. The crystal shape you decide to fill in must be symmetrical (identical on both sides when an imaginary line is drawn down the middle.) Any crystals presented on the grid are only valid if they are symmetrical.

3 You and your opponent take turns to color in the first square of your crystal, one square at a time, as the whole shape grows.

4 At the start of the game, it is probably best to scatter your squares widely across the grid to explore places where you could potentially develop crystals.

5 During the middle and final stages of the game, it's best to focus on smaller areas and concentrate on spreading a single crystal over a wide surface area.

6 Try to obstruct your opponent's crystals before they form.

7 The game continues until there are no squares left to fill.

8 To find out your scores, add the number of squares contained within each crystal.

9 The player with the highest number of squares (not crystals) wins the match.

96

Word Games

Antonyms

 2 or more   1   None

 To think of as many pairs of words that are opposites to each other.

1 Begin by saying a word. For example, "moon."

2 The other player needs to say a word that is its opposite, for example, "sun."

3 Whoever replies the quickest (and gives the correct answer) gets to choose the word for the next round.

4 If, at any time, someone says a word that has no opposite (for example, "nose,") the player who first realizes this will get first choice in the next round.

This game requires you to think real hard and give your partner words that are antonyms (the direct opposite of what he or she has said.)

Questions and Answers

 3 or more   2   Pencil and paper (for each player)

 To give answers to questions that preferably have no correct answer.

1 Each player writes down a question on a piece of paper like: "Why is the Earth round?" or "What came first: the chicken or the egg?"

2 Each player folds up his or her answers so no one can see them.

3 Collect the sheets of paper. Without unfolding them, mix them up, and hand one back to each player. He or she writes down an answer to an invisible question that he or she cannot see.

4 Unfold all the sheets and read out all the answers to the questions, one by one. These are bound to be very illogical so it's going to be crazy!

Picture Word Associations

  3 or more   2   Paper, pencil, and a picture or photograph cut out from a newspaper or magazine for each player

 To look at a picture you have never seen before and guess the same word associations that other players make.

1 Choose a photograph or an image. Cut it out from a newspaper or magazine without showing it to anyone. Everyone else does the same. Set a time limit for each round.

2 Place the piece of paper, pencil, and photograph (face down) in front of you on the table.

3 When it's your turn, turn the picture over so it's now face up. Everyone studies the image and are given a minute in which to list any words they can think of. For example, a picture of the sun might make you think of how thirsty you get in the heat. You might then think of something thirst-quenching like a cool glass of soda.

4 When the time is up, read out the words you wrote down, one by one.

5   The other players should shout out if any of their words match yours.

6   Keep track of the number of identical word picture associations made. Give yourself 1 point for every word match.

7   Any players who also shared the word association are also awarded 1 point.

8   When it's the second player's turn, he or she turns over his or her chosen picture, and the game carries on round the table.

9   Whoever has the highest number of word matches at the end of the rounds, wins.

Are you a mind reader? Play this entertaining picture word association game to find out!

Spelling Bee

 2 or more, plus an adult to be the "teacher"   2   A dictionary (optional)

To spell as many words correctly as possible.

1 Ask the "teacher" to prepare a list of words that matches everyone's spelling ability.

2 Players line up opposite each other (if in two teams).

3 The player farthest to your left is given a word to spell which he or she must first repeat, then spell out, then repeat again. For example, "balloon, B-A-L-L-O-O-N, balloon" etc.

4 If you spelled the word correctly, the next player is given a new word to spell. If not, he or she is given the chance to try the word that you got wrong, at which point you would be out and have to sit down.

5 The words get gradually harder and harder to spell.

6 Give one point for every word that's spelled correctly.

7 The last player (or teammate) to remain standing wins the contest.

This old-fashioned favorite develops word confidence. It's great fun either in or out of the classroom.

Earth, Wind, Air, and Fire

 6 or more 2 None

 To respond with the name of an animal, fish, or bird when the correct category is in play.

1 Stand in front of the other players. You can choose anyone at any time.

2 Point to someone and say "earth," "air," "fire," or "water," and count from 1 to 10 as fast as you can. If you say "earth," this person must name an animal before you reach 10. If you say "air," he or she must name a bird. If you call "water," he or she must name a fish. But if you call "fire," players must remain absolutely silent! Also, no two animals, birds, or fish can be the same in any one game.

3 You have three goes in total. Each time you mess up, you collect 1 point (for once, not a good thing!)

4 When you reach 3 points, you're out of the game.

5 Continue playing until there is a winner.

A fast-response game where little or no movement is required, but where you need to know when to keep quiet and when to speak out.

103

Word Factory

 2 or more   2   Pencil and paper (for each player)

 To make up the longest possible word from a series of eight letters.

1 Each player is given a some paper and a pencil.

2 Sit away from the other players so no one can see what you are writing down.

3 Take turns to call out a letter from the alphabet.

4 Everyone writes down these letters until eight have been called out.

5 You have 3 minutes to make up the longest possible word from these letters.

6 You can only use a letter once and your word can only be made up from the letters that were called out.

7 When the time limit is up, everyone calls out their individual word. Every letter is worth 1 point. The player with the longest word receives 5 points. The player who manages to use all eight letters wins 3 more points.

Use a dictionary if there's any doubt about whether the winning word exists or not!

Hangman

 3 or more   2   Pencil and paper

 To figure out the mystery word, letter by letter, before the hangman gets hung.

1 Think of a word and count the number of letters in it.

2 Draw a line of dashes, one for each letter in your word. For example, the word "schoolyard" would make 10 dashes.

3 Players take turns calling out letters of the alphabet. Write any correct letters down in the correct blank space (or blanks if it is repeated.) For example, on a word like "gorilla."

4 As the letters get filled in, players may also have a go at guessing the whole word.

5 If one of the players guesses a letter that's not part of the mystery word, write it down in a "scrap heap" on the side of the sheet of paper.

6 Start to draw the head of the hangman dangling from the gallows above the line of blanks. The gallows can be just a letter "L" upside down—it doesn't have to be anything fancy.

7 Each incorrect question adds another part to the drawing—a right arm, a left arm, and so on.

8 If players take a lot time to guess the word, they must continue suggesting letters until the hangman is complete—and they have lost.

9 The player who guesses the word before the figure is complete, wins.

This game has been played for many years and can get quite competitive.

Hidden Words

 2 or more   3   Pencil and paper for each player, a watch or timer, a dictionary

 To "see" as many hidden words inside a bigger word as quickly as you can.

1. Everyone agrees a key word with at least seven letters. For example, "kitchen."

2. Give yourself and the other players 5 minutes to study the word and come up with a series of mini words "hidden" inside the longer word. For example, inside the word "kitchen," you can find shorter words like "itch," "it," and "net." Any new words must contain at least two letters, and you can only use the given letters once.

3. Write down all the words you find.

4. The player with the longest list of words wins. He or she gets to pick the next word and the game continues.

Good spelling ability is key in this game.

Strategy Games

Giant Slaying

 2   1   A sheet of graph paper, a pencil, 3 white counters (the "dwarfs",) and 1 black counter (the "giant")

 To win, the white counters must trap the black counter in circle number 9. To win, the black counter must break behind their line and land on circle number 1.

1. Copy the game board shown below.

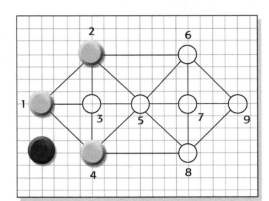

2. Place the white counters on circles 1, 2, and 4. The black counter can go on any of the circles, but you're not allowed to have more than one counter on a circle at a time.

3. The player with the white counters is first to play.

4. Players take turns to move each counter along the lines on the board toward any circles that are free. White counters can move sideways or forward, but not backward. The black counter, however, can be played in any direction.

5. The white counters win if they block the black counter in circle 9. The black counter wins if it reaches circle 1.

The Star

 2   1   A sheet of graph paper, a pencil, 4 white counters, 4 black counters

 To block all your opponent's counters so they cannot move.

1. Copy the game board shown below.

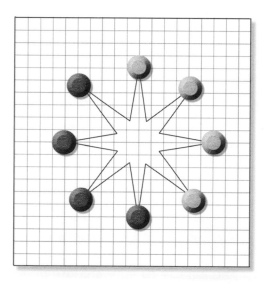

2. Place all eight counters on the tips of the arms of the star. The four black counters are placed on the left. The four white counters are placed on the right.

3. Draw lots or toss up to see who goes first.

4. A counter can move from the tip of the arm toward the middle (but only if one of the arms either side is already blocked by a counter of the opposite color,) or it can move from one arm of the star to the next if this space is free.

5. Two counters cannot be stacked in the same place on the game board.

6. The first player to block all of his or her opponent's counters is the winner.

Fox and Geese

 2   1   1 black counter, 13 white counters, graph paper, and a pencil

 If you control the single counter (the fox,) to try and remove all of the geese from the board by jumping them. If you control the 13 counters (the geese,) to prevent this by pinning down the fox so it cannot move.

1 Copy the cross-shaped game board shown below.

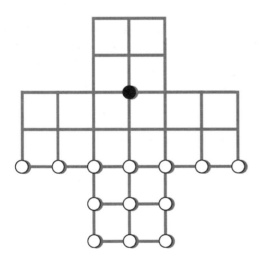

This game is a good introduction to checkers, which is a little more complicated. In it, the geese must work together to chase and trap the fox before they're captured. The sly fox must catch as many geese as it can to prevent it becoming trapped!

2 Place the counters as shown. The black counter is the fox. The 13 white counters are the geese.

3 Draw lots or toss up to decide who plays the black counter.

4 One of the white counters makes the opening move.

5 You and your opponent take turns to move your own counters forward, backward, and sideways (but not diagonally.)

6 If you're the fox, your task is to break through the line of geese and gobble them up all the way to the back row. The fox can capture a goose by jumping over it to an empty square beyond. The counter must then be removed from the board. If there is the opportunity for a sequence of multiple hops, the fox can capture more than one goose in one go!

7 If you're playing the geese, you cannot capture the fox, but you can corner it on all sides so it's unable to move in any direction!

Two-Color Snakes

 2   1   Graph paper, 2 color pencils

 To stop your opponent's slithering snake in its tracks.

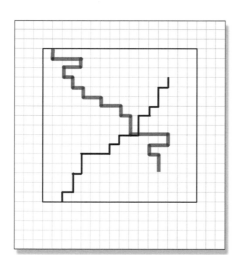

4 You and your opponent take turns to start drawing your snakes from opposite sides of the paper.

1 Box in a large grid (16 x 16 squares) on the graph paper.

2 Each player is given a pencil.

3 Draw lots or toss up to see who goes first.

5 You start to draw a continuous line only by connecting one horizontal or vertical side of a square at a time—no more than that is allowed in one go.

6 The first player to block his or her opponent's snake by touching it is the winner.

Connect the Dots

 2 or more   2   Graph paper, a pencil or crayon (for each player)

 To close off as many squares on the board as you can by completing boxes using horizontal or vertical connecting lines.

1 Copy the grid below. The number of dots does not matter, but make sure you have the same number of dots going across as going down.

2 Each player is given a pencil or crayon.

3 Draw lots or toss up to see who goes first.

4 Connect the first two dots with a vertical line.

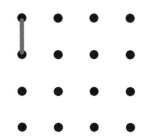

5 When it's your opponent's turn, he or she connects another two dots with a horizontal line this time.

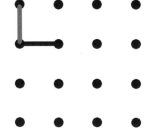

6 Following your opponent's move, connect one of these dots to a new dot with another vertical line.

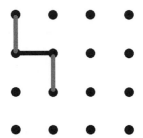

7 Your opponent responds by connecting two more dots, with a vertical line this time.

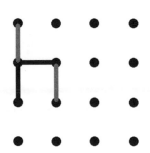

8 When you close off the first box in the game, write your initials inside (shown here as AA.) It's still your turn.

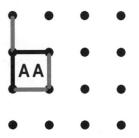

9 Add another horizontal line to connect two more dots.

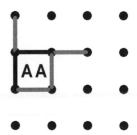

10 Continue to play until the grid is full and there's nowhere left to go.

11 Whoever has the most boxes to his or her name at the end of the game wins.

Battleships

 2   3   A sheet of graph paper and a felt-tip (for each player)

 To find and sink your opponent's navy before your fleet is found and sunk.

1 Divide your sheet of paper into two halves with two game grids—one at the top and one at the bottom. Each grid must measure 10 squares tall by 10 squares wide. Make sure your opponent's grid looks the same as yours.

2 Label the first row of squares along the top of both grids with the letters A–J. Then label the first rows of squares running vertically down the sides with the numbers 1 to 10. This is your battleground.

3 Mark the positions of your fleet in the top grid: an aircraft carrier is five squares in a straight line; two battleships or destroyers are four squares in a straight line; and five submarines are a single square each. Remember the different ships can be placed anywhere on the grid (either horizontally or vertically) but their edges must not touch.

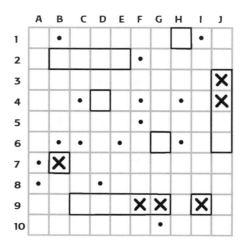

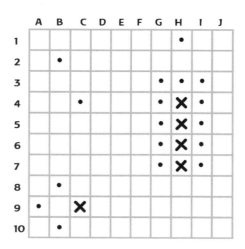

4 You and your opponent take turns to call out different grid positions using a letter and a number. If, for example, he or she says B7 (see top diagram,) one of your four boats has been hit and sunk as it only occupied one square. You must

then reply "hit and sunk," mark it with an "X," and say which craft it was. In this case, the other player gets to have another go. If, for example, G3 was called out instead, you would say "water" and it would be your turn.

5 Record your opponent's hits and misses in the top grid. Mark any hits with an "X" and misses with a dot. Record your hits and misses against your opponent's fleet in the bottom grid in the same way.

6 The first player to sink all of his or her opponent's ships is the winner.

This classic game of strategy lets you direct your own naval battle and play for your opponent's targets!

Checkers

  2   3   A checker or chessboard, 12 white checkers, 12 black checkers, a piece of paper, and a pencil (if you want to keep track of the score)

 To capture all of your opponent's checkers, or block them so they cannot move.

1 Set up all 24 checkers on the first three rows of black squares on opposite sides of the board. If you're playing the black checkers, you move first.

2 Single checkers move forward diagonally, one square at a time. Each player takes a turn to move one of his or her checkers.

3 You can capture one of your opponent's checkers by jumping over it and landing your checker on the empty square beyond.

4 If one of your checkers is next to one that belongs to your opponent and the square beyond it is free, you must jump over this checker. Remove it from the board.

5 It's possible to do multiple jumps as well—the same checker can jump several times to capture more than one piece in a row, if there are empty squares diagonally behind each.

6 If you touch a checker, you have to move it. So, if you're not going to play it, remember not to touch it.

7 When you move your checker to the last row on the opposite side of the board, that checker becomes a king. If you place another checker on top of it (to crown it) this piece can now move diagonally forwards, or backwards. You're allowed to jump as many of your opponent's checkers on the same move as possible.

8 The player who first captures all his or her opponent's pieces is the winner.

3-D Noughts and Crosses

 2 3 Paper and pencil, a ruler

 To score four symbols in a row across more than one face on a three-dimensional cube.

1 Draw a cube. Divide each face into nine squares.

2 Draw lots or toss up to decide who gets to be the noughts and who gets to be the crosses.

3 You and your opponent take turns to mark one square at a time with either an "O" (nought) or an "X" (cross.) You can strike through a line horizontally, vertically, or diagonally. Your challenge is to stop your opponent from out thinking you.

4 If you line up four noughts (or crosses) across more than one cube face, you have beaten your opponent and are the winner.

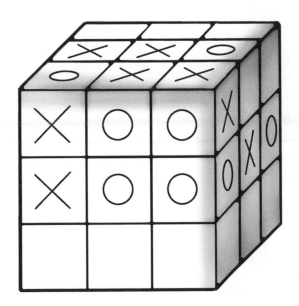

This solid game of strategy is a three-dimensional version of tick-tack-toe!

119

Halma

 2
want

3

10 white counters, 10 black counters, graph paper, and a pencil (if you to keep track of the score)

 To move all your counters from your corner into the opposite corner of the board.

1 Copy the game board shown below.

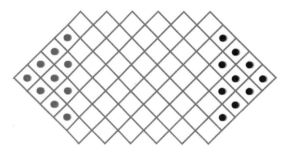

2 Position the white and black counters on opposite corners of the board.

3 You and your opponent take turns to move your own counters. On each turn, you can move a counter into the next square or, if possible, hop over another counter into the square beyond, and

so on. The game starts to become interesting when there are lots of counters in the middle of the board.

4 Counters can move forwards, backward, and diagonally. A single counter can also make multiple hops over several other counters and quickly move across the board.

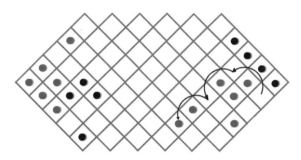

5 No counters may be captured or removed.

6 You can jump over your own counters as well as those of the other player.

7 The first player to move all of his or her counters into the opponent's corner is the winner.

This challenging game of strategy was originally played on a huge game board that was 16 squares x 16 squares (256 squares in total). Just think, a standard chess or checkerboard only has 64!

Tabletop Games

Dominoes

 2   2   A standard set of 28 dominoes

 To lay down as many dominoes as possible by matching the number of dots on their faces.

1 Find a table or another flat surface like the floor. Place all **28** dominoes face down and mix them up.

2 Each player draws one domino from this "bone pile." Whoever gets the highest scoring ("heaviest") domino goes first.

3 Each player takes seven dominoes from the "bone pile."

4 Set up your hand in a row with the seven pieces standing upright so no one can see their value.

5 If you're the first player, lay any domino face up in the middle of the table. The person to your left goes next.

6 He or she selects a domino piece from his or her hand. It must have the same number of dots on one side as the piece on the table.

7 When you're making the numbers match, place your domino against another piece so that the ends with the same number of dots are touching.

8 Any player with a double can play one end of this (or any other matching) domino but must place their "double" domino across the bottom of the original piece in a T-shape. This is how you build up the famous domino pattern.

9 If you have no matches for what's on the table, keep taking from the "bone pile" until you find a piece that you can play.

10 The next player takes a turn and plays a matching piece or takes from the "bone pile" as well, and so on.

11 If the player before you has played a double, you can continue the layout by jumping over the "T" in the pattern or playing off in one of the directions of the "T."

12 Whoever gets rid of all his or her dominoes first is the winner. If the "bone pile" runs out before anyone has used up all their pieces, the player with the lowest number of dots wins.

Get ready to match up numbers in this classic tabletop challenge. These flat, rectangular tiles are usually black but also come in white. One face is divided by a line with one, two, three, four, five, six dots, or a blank space on either side of it. The dots either side of the line are called "suits." Tiles with an equal number of dots on either side of the line are called one-number suits and are doubles. There are seven of these in a standard 28-tile set. The remaining 21 dominoes are mixed suits with a different number of dots on either side of the line, or dots on one side and a blank on the other.

Pick-Up Sticks

 2 or more

 3

 40 thin pencil sticks (10 inches or about 25 centimeters in length,) red, blue, yellow, and green paint, a pencil sharpener, a paintbrush

 To pull out as many sticks as you can during your turn without moving the others in the pile—easier said than done!

1 Sharpen each pencil end using the sharpener. Paint 20 yellow, 12 red, five blue, three green, and the other two with spirals in a color of your choice. The pick-up sticks should look like huge, color toothpicks.

2 At the start of the game, hold all the sticks in both hands, keeping them vertical to the hard surface of a desk or a table. Set the bottom of one hand on the table so that the sticks rise straight up. Open your other hand and gently let the sticks fall.

3 Players take turns to try to pick up one of the sticks without moving the others in the pile. If the stick you're trying to pull out moves something else even by a fraction, it's the next player's turn. If their luck holds, they'll keep on pulling out sticks until the pile finally jiggles.

4 Players can only add up their score once all sticks have been removed. Yellow sticks are worth 3 points; red sticks are worth 5 points; blue sticks are worth 10 points; green sticks are worth 15 points; and the spiral ones (where the big points are) are each worth 20!

This game requires a steady hand, concentration, and a high tolerance for frustration!

125

Pick-Up Toothpicks

 2 or more   3   A box of toothpicks

 To pick up the last toothpick on the table using some serious strategic maneuvers.

1 Find a table or another flat surface.

2 Use any number of toothpicks.

3 Divide them up into as many piles as you want. You don't have to count the number of toothpicks in each pile—this doesn't matter.

4 You and your opponent take turns picking up one, some, or all the toothpicks in one pile. But here's the twist—when it's your turn, you can also choose to *divide* an existing pile into two or more piles instead.

5 Players cannot pick up pieces from more than one pile or divide more than one pile in a single turn.

6 Try to think several moves ahead of your opponent. For example, if there are two piles on the table, you might not want to pick up one pile in one go because your opponent can then pick up the other and win the game. It's a better gaming tactic, for example, to pick up *some* of one pile or divide it into two piles or more.

7 The player who's left with the final move is the winner.

Card Games

Old Maid

 3 to 6   1   A standard deck of 52 cards

 To collect card pairs and avoid the "old maid" (the Queen of Spades.)

1. Find a table or another flat surface on which to play.

2. Take out the other three queens from the deck but leave in the Queen of Spades (the "old maid.")

3. Everyone picks a card. Whoever selects the highest card gets to be the dealer. If you're the dealer, shuffle the deck and deal the cards, face down, one at a time, to the other players. Some players might get more cards than others—this is normal in the game.

4. Players look at the cards they've been dealt, pull out any matching pairs (in terms of rank,) and lay down any matches in a pile next to them.

5. If you draw a card that matches the one in your hand, lay the pair in a pile face up. If you have no pair, play continues with the player to your left. If you have three cards that match in number, put two down and keep the third. If you have four cards, you can put down two pairs.

6. After everyone has finished laying down their matches, the first player to your left fans out the cards in his or her hand, keeping the faces hidden. The player to this person's left picks out a card and hopes to match it with what is in his or her hand. Any matches go in the pile.

7. Play goes round in a circle with players picking cards from each other and laying down matches.

8. There is only one "old maid" card, and it can never make a pair. Whoever has it can therefore never win the game!

9. The first player to end up without any cards wins.

10. The player left holding the Queen of Spades in his or her hand is the (very) unlucky loser!

Success in this game is about pure luck and has nothing to do with skill. It's a level playing field from the start.

Slapjack

 2 to 5   1   A standard deck of 52 cards

 To win all the cards by quickly recognizing the Jacks when they appear before another card gets slapped down on top.

1 Find a table or another flat surface on which to play. Put the deck on the table in front of you.

2 Everyone picks a card. Whoever selects the highest card is the dealer. He or she shuffles and deals the deck, face down, one card at a time, to the other players. Some players might get more cards than others—this is normal.

3 Place all your cards face down. Every other player does the same.

4 If you're to the dealer's left you go first. Turn over the top card from your pile in front of everyone. The player to your left then places his or her card face up on top of your original card. As the game continues, new cards are always being added to this central pile until someone lays down a Jack.

5 As soon you see the Jack, slap your hand down on it before someone else does. If you beat the other players to it, take the pile of cards underneath the Jack. Mix it with your pile.

6 The player to your left starts a new pile of cards in the middle of the table. If you move too quickly and slap another card by mistake, you have to give one of your cards to each of the other players.

7 Whoever runs out of cards before the game is over is out.

8 The first player to collect all the cards is the winner.

You must have lightning-fast reactions and the eyes of a hawk to slap down the Jack and win all the cards lying underneath!

Fifteen

 1 2 A standard deck of 52 cards, plus Jokers

 To be an ace at this game of skilled calculation, you must select any number of random cards to try to score 15 points as often as you can, until all the cards in the reserve pile have been used up.

1 Sit at a table. Shuffle the deck and deal out 16 cards in four rows, face down, four cards to a row. The remaining cards go in a reserve pile to one side.

2 From the 16 cards that are laid out face down on the table, turn over as many cards as you need to get 15 points (or as close to this score as possible.) Do this as many times as you can. You cannot go over a score of 15 points or you have lost.

The value of the different cards is as follows:

- Joker (15 points)
- King (13 points)
- Queen (12 points)
- Jack (11 points)
- other cards are worth the number of points they represent (for example, the 10 of Spades is worth 10 points, and so on).

3 Cards that are used up go in a waste pile. As you play, replace them with cards from the reserve pile and continue to play until you are unable to collect 15 points from the cards that are left over. See how long your luck holds out!

War

 2   2   A standard deck of 52 cards, watch or timer

 To capture all of your opponent's cards.

1 Find a table or another flat surface on which to play. Set the timer.

2 You and your opponent each pick a card. The person who selects the higher card gets to shuffle and deal out the deck, face down, one card at a time.

3 You and your opponent place your cards in a pile, face down, in front of each other.

4 Turn your top cards over together and place them face up and side by side in the middle. (Remember that Aces are high-scoring cards in this game.)

5 If you play the higher ranking card, you get to keep both cards (and vice versa.)

6 Collect these cards and add them to the bottom of your stack.

7 If you both turn over cards of the same rank, you declare "war" on each other and the fun part begins.

8 Each one of you places the three top cards from your pile face down on top of the card you have just declared war with.

9 Each one of you then places a fourth card on top of the three cards, face up. The higher face-up card wins all the cards. If your cards and those of your opponent match once again, it's "double war."

10 The card battle continues until the winner captures all 52 cards. You can also win if your opponent runs out of cards.

Why win one battle when you can win the whole war? Do make sure you give yourself a time limit as this game of chance can carry on for ages!

Chase the Ace

 5 or more   2   A standard deck of 52 cards, 3 counters (or buttons) for each player

 To get rid of the Ace (the lowest card.)

1. Everyone picks a card. Whoever chooses the highest card deals the first round. He or she is the dealer.

2. The dealer hands each player three counters (each one represents a "life" in the game.)

3. Everyone puts a "stake" (a quantity of their counters—not all!) in the pot (to be collected by the winner of that round.)

4. Each player is dealt one card face down by the dealer. Everyone looks at their card and decides whether they want to keep it or trade it (if it's a low-ranking card) when it's their turn. Any undealt cards are left in a pile on the table.

5. The player left of the dealer goes first and play continues round the table in a clockwise direction. Each player can either keep a card ("stand,") or trade it with the first person to their left and hope for a better one ("change.") The player who has just been forced to trade decides whether to "stand" or "change," and so on. Changing a card is a big risk—unless you already hold an Ace, it's very likely you will end up with a lower card. If you trade and the new card is an Ace, a 2, or a 3, you must tell the other players.

6. To trade a card, simply slide it face down over to the player on your left. This person has to accept the swap unless he or she has a King, in which case the card is exposed and you must trade with the next player over. Players continue to be on the lookout for Aces as these will keep moving round the table.

7. The dealer's turn comes last and he or she cannot trade with anyone. To trade, he or she buries the card in the middle of the deck and chooses another card from the top of the pile and shows it to the other players. If you've picked a King and are the dealer, for example, you lose your hand and one counter.

8. The other players' cards are revealed. The player with the lowest card loses a counter.

9 If two players or more tie for the lowest card, each loses a life.

10 The player on the original dealer's left now becomes the dealer in the second round. Cards from the last round are added to the bottom of the deck and another hand is dealt.

11 Any player who loses all three lives is out of the game.

12 The last player with one remaining counter wins and collects the rewards in the pot.

What happens if both or all of the players that are left over tie for the lowest card, so they're all out of the game? Choose your favorite solution:

a They become joint winners and split the pot between them.

b They get to keep their last "life" and another round is played out between them.

c As the result is undecided, the pot is carried forward to the next game with each player adding a new stake to it.

In this betting and trading game, Kings are high and Aces are low. Suits don't count, and the cards rank in this order: King (high), Queen, Jack, 10, 9, 8, 7, 6, 5, 4, 3, 2, Ace (low.) Enjoy the thrill of collecting a pot after a winning round!

Rummy

 2 to 6   3   A standard deck of 52 cards

 To get rid of all your cards. To do this, you must find and collect certain card combinations (known as "melds") and lay off as many of your opponents' card combinations as possible.

1 Find a table or another flat surface on which to play. Place the card deck in front of you.

2 Everyone picks a card. The person who selects the highest card gets to shuffle and deal one card at a time, face down, to you and the others. He or she is the dealer. With two players playing, you each get 10 cards. If there are three to four players, each person receives seven cards; if there are five or six people around the table, each gets six cards.

3 Place the remaining cards in a stock pile face down in the middle of the table. Turn the top card face up and set it down by the first stack as a waste pile.

4 To win, try and collect as many melds as you possibly can—they will obviously change and have to be adjusted during the course of the game, depending on which cards everyone else is trying to collect.

5 The player to the dealer's left picks up the top card from either the stock pile or the waste pile. He or she discards any card from his or her hand onto the waste pile.

6 If you pick a card from this pile, you cannot put down the same card.

7 The game continues in a clockwise direction with each player picking up and discarding a card on their turn.

8 When you have a meld, you can either hold back or lay them face up on the table in full view of the other players. They can then lay their cards onto your melds by adding a fourth card to a three-of-a-kind, or to the high or low end of a three-in-a-row sequence.

9 Try to lay down as many cards as you can when it's your turn.

10 When the stock pile runs out and a player refuses the top card from the waste pile, flip it over and play it as new stock. Try to win your hand by playing all your cards, but you don't have to discard them when you go out unless you want to.

11 The first hand is scored, and the value of all the cards that are left over in the other players' hands are also added to it.

Cards are worth as follows:

- **Aces** – 1 point
- **Face cards, such as the jack, queen and king** – 10 points
- **Number cards** – their number value

12 The second hand is shuffled and dealt by the player on the dealer's left, and so on.

13 The game continues until a player reaches the points target that was decided before the game began, or until the agreed number of deals has been played.

There are probably more versions of rummy out there than any other card game. Players must have good strategic thinking and be able to rethink tactics while they watch the other players closely.

Tips for playing rummy

- On each turn, try doubling your score early by putting out all your cards (going rummy.) To do this, you cannot have laid out any melds or laid down any cards on your opponents' melds up to that point.

- Discard unwanted face cards.

- During any game, watch how your opponents are playing their cards and try not to discard cards that might be useful to the player on your left. Start keeping track of which cards others need and avoid helping them out.

- Don't be afraid to change your strategy halfway through if you notice others seem to be snatching up the cards you need. They might be onto you, too! For maximum success, keep a clear head and be prepared to keep changing the groups and sequences that you're collecting…

- Remember to try and keep your score low by not holding onto high-ranking cards at the end of a game.

What is a meld? Melds include any three or four cards of the same rank or suit. For example, four 6s or three Queens make a meld, as do the 2, 3 and 4 of Clubs. The Ace is a low card in this game: it can go before a 2 or a 3 in a sequence, but not after a King.

Dice Games

Little Pig

 2 or more   1   Pencil and paper (for each player), colored crayons, 2 dice

 With a little luck, you may be the first to finish your drawing.

To draw/color in the eye, 2.
To draw/color in the snout, 3.
To draw/color in the ears, 4.
To draw/color in the legs, 5.
To draw/color in the tail, 6. You really need to think lucky if you are to finish the drawing of your pig at all!

1 Look at the drawing of the pig. Each part of it corresponds to a number. You can only draw the part that corresponds to the number that comes up on each throw of the dice when it's your turn.

2 To be able to draw/color in the body of the pig, you must throw a dice combination that adds up to 9.

3 For example, if you've drawn all the parts except the tail, you must score 6 on the next throw, or your opponent could have better luck and beat you to it!

4 The first player to complete their animal is the winner.

Nifty Fifty

 2 or more 1 2 dice, pencil and paper (for scores)

 To be the first player to reach 50 points by rolling two dice.

1 Find a table or another flat surface. Make sure all players are sitting down.

2 Roll a die beforehand to see who starts the game. Whoever gets the highest number goes first. The second highest score gets to go second, and so on. A tie is broken by another roll of the die.

3 Players take turns to shoot the dice and aim for doubles.

4 The rolls are worth as follows: all dice doubles score 5 points (except 3s and 6s); double 6s are worth a massive 25 points so, obviously, trying to aim for these is a smart move. Very important: avoid unlucky double 3s if you can, as they wipe out your score up to that point and you have to restart.

5 Use pencil and paper to keep track of each other's scores.

6 The game continues with each player taking one roll on every turn.

7 The first player to reach a score of 50 points or over wins.

As a general rule of thumb, try to shoot dice doubles (the same number on each cube face) to get ahead in this game but avoid rolling two 3s!

The Racing Clock

 3 or 4   2   2 die

 To go "around the clock" by rolling numbers 1 to 12 in the correct order.

1 Find a table or another flat surface. Make sure all players are sitting down.

2 Roll a die beforehand to see who starts the game. If you get the highest number, you go first. Whoever has the second highest score gets to go second, and so on. A tie is broken by another roll of the die.

3 Roll the dice once, aiming to get 1 on both faces. If you're unlucky, you'll have to hope for better luck next time as you wait for your turn again. If you roll successfully, you can shoot for a 2 on your next turn. What's really exciting is that you can try to get a 2 in one of two ways: either on a single die, or with the right combination of dice.

4 If you get this total, you can shoot for 3 at your next turn, gradually working your way up to 12 during the course of the game. Like the hands on a clock!

5 If luck is on your side and you manage to score two of the numbers that you need for the sequence with a single roll, you can count them both. For example, if you're aiming for the 5 in the sequence, rolling both a 5 and a 6 at the same time counts. Then, at your next turn, you can skip straight to 7!

6 After 6, it's obvious you need to roll a combination of dice for numbers 7 to 12.

7 The game continues with you and your opponent taking turns until one player manages to complete going "around the clock" before the others.

Depending on how lucky you (or the other players) are on the day, this game could wrap up quite quickly!

Multiplication Dice

 3 or more   3   3 dice, pencil, and paper (for scores)

 To reach the highest possible score by rolling not two but three dice. There is a twist, however...

1 Find a table or another flat surface. Make sure all players are sitting down.

2 Roll a die beforehand to see who starts the game. If you obtain the highest number, you get to go first. Whoever has the second highest score gets to go second, and so on. A tie is broken by another roll of the die.

3 Roll the three dice in one throw and put the one that scores the highest to one side. If the highest number comes up on two dice, set one die aside. If the same number comes up on all three dice, select only one die. The two remaining dice are then rolled again and the highest-scoring die gets chosen. The last die is now rolled.

4 To tally up your score, add the numbers on the first two dice and multiply this sum by the value of the third die. For example, if you get a 3 and 4 on the first two dice and a 5 on the third, you do a quick calculation like this: $(3 + 4) \times 5$.

Your score is 35 points because you add up the first two numbers and get 7, then multiply it by 5 to get 35.

5 You can play this game for as many rounds as you wish, but remember to always watch the score.

6 The player with the highest total score is the winner.

Look out for the power of the third roll. It's very unpredictable and can make or break a player in the last stages of this game!

143

Unlucky Dice

 2 or more 3 5 dice, pencil and paper (for scores)

To collect as many points as possible as you get rid of the "unlucky" dice.

1 Find a table or another flat surface. Make sure both players are sitting down.

2 Roll a die beforehand to see who starts the game. The player with the lowest score gets to go first this time. If there's a tie, break it with another roll of the die.

3 Players take turns rolling all five dice. If no 2 or 5 comes up, you can add up the numbers on the faces of the five dice to get your score. These are the points scored on a single roll.

4 If either a 2 or a 5 (or both) come up, you score nothing and must remove the "unlucky" die or dice before the next roll. You could also have rolled "lucky" and kept all five dice intact. Depending on your luck, you could at this stage have five, four, or three dice, for example.

5 On each successive roll, players continue trying to add points to their scores or eliminate the "unlucky" dice until all five dice are "dead" and the game is over.

6 Whoever has the most points after everyone else has dropped out, wins.

Whatever you roll, try to avoid 2 or 5 in your throw!